# THE PUBLIC STYLE:

## A STUDY OF THE COMMUNITY PARTICIPATION OF PROTESTANT MINISTERS

by

Walter M. Stuhr, Jr.

Printed in the United States of America



Center for the Scientific Study of Religion
5757 University Avenue
Chicago, Illinois 60637

I S B N: 0-913348-02-3

Library of Congress Catalog Card Number: 72-89687

## TABLE OF CONTENTS

TABLE OF CONTENTS (continued)

## ACKNOWLEDGMENTS

First I must thank the 105 parish ministers, men who, in the spring of 1967, contributed to this study by taking time to write and talk about their ministry. It is hoped that this study in turn can make some contribution to their continuing ministry in "the church on location."

Dr. Gibson Winter of the University of Chicago Divinity School was my chief advisor throughout my graduate program which culminated in this study. He provided both criticism and encouragement, at the right time and in the right proportion. Dr. Alvin Pitcher of the Divinity School and Dr. Brian Berry of the Center for Urban Studies have given valuable assistance.

Four of my colleagues in the Ethics and Society Department of the Divinity School, Richard Hoehn, Talbot Shaw, Wesley Wilkie, and Lawrence Witmer, collaborated with me in designing and administering the research instruments. The weekly interchange that took place in the Community Organization Research Colloquium with these and other colleagues helped to shape and sharpen the subject matter for the research.

A number of persons and institutions provided funds, consultation, and other services at various crucial points along the way: the Center for the Scientific Study of Religion, Chicago, which is also publishing this monograph; Dr. Thomas Crawford, social psychologist at the University of Chicago; the Pacific Lutheran Theological Seminary, Berkeley, California; Ed Hutchinson of the Bureau of Community Research, Berkeley; the Survey Research Center, University of California, Berkeley; Dr. Eugene Willeke, Stanford University; and Mrs. Sheldon Allman, Chicago.

My wife Barbara agonized with me throughout, and typed endlessly. She and Deborah, Rebecca, and Philip together supplied the necessary extra motivation to see the project through to completion.



Walter Stuhr
Pacific Lutheran Theological Seminary
Berkeley, California
January, 1972

## LIST OF TABLES

# CHAPTER I

## PARTICIPATION AND THE QUESTION OF STYLE

### Introduction

This monograph is concerned with the style of participation of Protestant parish ministers in their own parish communities. As such it is intended to contribute to the broader concern of the relationship of churches to society. The assumption is that the minister personifies the meeting point for the societal and theological pressures experienced by the churches. He is the official representative of the church "on location." By training and expectation he is the chief instrument of the church's task.

The direction of the churches' participation in society ought to be evident in the parish minister's own style of participation in his immediate social situation. To be sure, the minister is not the church; therefore, one cannot generalize from the minister to the church as a whole. On the other hand, if what we expect of churches generally is not observable in their professional leaders, our expectations lack validity.

Two differing styles of participation are proposed at the outset. One we will call the parochial style. It is participation in society through and primarily on behalf of the congregation and its denominational organization. The minister's preaching, teaching, and organizing have their social implications and effects, but are not undertaken explicitly for that purpose. The parochial style implies that within society as a whole the churches have a specific sphere of responsibility. The minister's task is to see that it is carried out. He moves beyond that sphere only at the request of other institutions, such as the government, in order to undergird them in their spheres of responsibility. The parochial style then tends to locate the minister within the social establishment, and to see the task of the church as harmonious with that of the larger social system.

The other style we call the public style. In the public style the minister moves outside the church's own structure to participate in society. His actions both within the church and in the general community are directed specifically at affecting the public well-being. It is participation in the public eye, subject not only to public approval but also to public criticism. It is prepared to move beyond the socially expected sphere of responsibility. The public style may locate the minister outside of the social establishment, and the task of the church may even set it in opposition to the larger social system.

In the following pages we present the sociological and theological background against which these styles must be evaluated. This will be followed by the presentation of empirical data which can both more fully characterize these styles, and provide some indication as to which of the styles is most observable in contemporary ministry.

## SOCIOLOGICAL BACKGROUND

### Urbanization

To live in American society is to live in a condition of change. And it is in the metropolitan areas that the evidence of change is especially apparent: physical deterioration; redistribution of population, both geographically and demographically; the shifting of the frontier from land to technology; challenge to accepted ways of believing, of behaving, of arranging and regulating the lives of individuals and groups.

A concept which includes all of these manifestations of change is "urbanization": the gathering of the population into the cities, which have become metropolitan centers and are becoming megalopoli. Urbanization also refers to the way in which society is structured to carry on its business of supporting and regulating its own life and the life of its constituency. Structure is therefore a key factor in the way change is channeled and experienced; and the evidence indicates that the structures which largely determine the way in which change is channeled and experienced are becoming more concentrated in location and more extended in controlling influence.[1]

Urbanization also underscores the contemporary role of man as principal social agent. For much of his history man has tended to see the content and ordering of life as more or less fixed. Where change took place it was thought to be through the agency of the gods or fate, or the inexorable working of natural law or the forces of historical evolution. Man's role was limited to suffering the results of, or at best cooperating with, change. Man's role as initiator, however, has been emerging with increasing clarity. This is partly a consequence of the demythologizing of nature and history to reveal man's agency in what has already come to pass. It is partly a consequence of coming to understand the structure and process of nature and history as providing conditions which enable rather than limit human agency.

The existing limits upon what man can accomplish, therefore, now are seen as temporary barriers to be overcome by continuing research and experimentation, not as fixed in the nature of things. The contemporary acknowledgment of man's agency expresses itself in the sophisticated structuring into industry of research and development, the appointment of Presidential commissions to investigate causes of critical social conditions, and the allocation of blame or praise for things as they are to various individuals, groups, and agencies. In the words of e. e. cummings, "A world of made is not a world of born."[2] Contemporary society, especially in its urban manifestation, is a world which increasingly can be built to man's specifications; it does not come ready-formed to natural or divine specifications.

In industry and to a lesser extent in government, specific goals are set, research is carried on and decisions are made and implemented; and to the extent that this process is successful, the accompanying change is intentional. But what is not intended or not intentionally taken into consideration is the consequences of these very specialized successes for the general state of society as the common life of man. Corporate power and profit predominate as criteria for decision and action, not general human well-being. The assumption has been that what is good according to the former criteria, will also be good according to the latter. Present conditions, most dramatically the ecological crisis, do not support that assumption.

There are those persons who appear obviously to be the "victims" of society. Their stories are documented on the front pages of the newspapers, as well as in scholarly articles. Probably the majority of the public, however, feels the condition in a less conscious way. Theirs is more a general malaise in their day to day living. The rising voice of the so-called "silent majority" or "forgotten man" indicates that the number of those who feel that "all is well" is steadily diminishing.

There is both the outward appearance and the inner sense that change must be intentionally controlled in order to ensure the quality of our common life. In the local residential community, people seem most keenly aware of the lack of control. The local community also happens to be the site of the parish church and therefore the basic place of ministry for the parish minister, who is the particular focus of our attention.

The urgent social need for control of change raises the problem of how such control is to be affected. Any theory or strategy of social control, in the light of the above discussion, must meet the following criteria: it must take into account the condition of change; it must provide for the agency of man; it must include general human well-being as an essential point of consideration. A theory which meets these criteria is proposed by Amitai Etzioni in his article "Toward a Theory of Societal Guidance."[3] In Etzioni's terminology the foregoing description of urbanization corresponds to that of an "ongoing society," i.e., a society which does not allow for adequate collective societal control, which is characterized more by "drift" than by intentional direction. On the other hand, the society which can exercise control over the forces of change is a "self-transforming" society. The need for social control might then be re-stated as the need for social transformation.

Etzioni proposes three conditions as essential for the self-transforming society. The first condition is that of "cybernetic capacity." Cybernetic capacity is the ability to collect, process (come to conclusions), and use (introduce into the decision-making and implementation process) knowledge.

Etzioni's use of "knowledge" implies more than scientific fact-gathering and analysis, although that is certainly included. It is evaluative as well as cognitive knowledge. Neither the validity of the system in relation to the values, nor the values themselves is assumed as a given. Both, facts and values, are relevant to social decision-making. Thus the knowledge "input" components of society would include both the sciences and the humanities. It would also require relative independence from and at the same time structured access to the decision-making component.

The second condition for the self-transforming society is the "decision-making and power-mobilization capacity." There must be the social capacity to make policy and to allocate the assets of society to collective action. Here the agency of man in social control is clear. If society is to move in certain directions, decisions must be made and action taken so that the multiplicity of social forces and interests are channeled appropriately. There is neither an "unseen hand" nor a congruence or balance of interests that can be counted upon to guarantee a self-transforming society.

The third condition for an active society is the "consensus formation capacity." This is the ability to mobilize maximum public support for social policy. Conscious attention to this function is required since social control generates alienation in those who are controlled. As alienation increases, so does the number of social assets that must be allocated to achieving compliance, and the number available for constructive action decreases. Therefore, although some conflict of given preferences of the public with the guided efforts of the elite is assumed, the universal availability of knowledge input should generate a significant degree of congruence between the given preferences and the guided efforts.

The dynamic characteristic of Etzioni's conditions of cybernetic capacity and decision-making and power-mobilization capacity is therefore extended to the consensus formation capacity. Consensus is not a given; it is constructed. The criterion of social intentionality in behalf of general human well-being is met implicitly, therefore, in the structured approach to control and in grounding the control in the broadest base possible, i.e., the social whole.

Etzioni's framework for a self-transforming society is a useful tool for understanding and responding to the American societal situation as we have described it. For the further purposes of this study the three conditions are stated alternately as follows. The cybernetic capacity is the sensitizing function through which society is made aware of changes and values which impinge upon the short-range effectiveness as well as the long-range validity and viability of the routine social life.

The decision-making and power-mobilizing capacity is the politicizing function. Through this function the collective intentions, which represent potential control, are translated into collective actions. The politicizing function is carried out primarily but not exclusively by the "elite." The appropriateness or necessity of this function being fulfilled by non-elite organizations is also allowed for.

The consensus-forming capacity is the legitimating function, by which control receives broad support, including public consent, participation, and appropriate complementary activity. These functions or capacities are all interdependent. The legitimating function, for instance, is not understood as an arm of the politicizing function, but as both a check upon and a facilitator of it. Selectivity is assumed in the legitimating function.

The key to controlling change, or social transformation, is a realistic, rational, and responsible process of social policy-formation and implementation. The emphasis is on the politicizing function, which directly effects formation and implementation. This must become an ordered, intentional process. But in order that it be more than rational, it must be informed by the realities of the policy-formation and implementation situation, and responsible to those whose lives are affected by the policy; thus it is necessary that the sensitizing and legitimating functions be joined with the politicizing function.

## THEOLOGICAL BACKGROUND

### Loyalty to the Kingdom of God

The Protestant parish minister (hereafter designated as the "minister") by virtue of his occupation, holds a committed position; in the carrying out of this position there is a referrent which transcends society as it is. His role is theologically as well as socially conditioned. The Protestant churches are the institutional base of the ministers, both for defining their theological commitment and for conditioning the everyday carrying out of their vocation. Therefore it is to the churches, especially in their American manifestation, that we now turn.

In The Kingdom of God in America, H. Richard Niebuhr proposes the concept of the kingdom of God as the theological principle for interpreting the Protestant movement generally, and American Protestantism particularly. The kingdom of God is the rulership of God in the realm of being. Niebuhr proposes three characteristics of this principle as developed in Protestantism: primacy, immediacy, and nearness.

The primacy of the kingdom indicates that among the claims of rulership in the realm of being, God's rulership has priority, both in initiative and in authority. This might be called the objective characteristic of the kingdom. As such it functions as the "center" of the Protestant movement.

The subjective characteristic is that of immediacy. All constituents of the realm of being, both individuals and institutions, are directly responsible to God. Not only is God's rulership asserted as present reality, but a "confession of the sole rulership of God and the declaration of loyalty to his kingdom"[4] is called for on the part of constituent parts. No person or institution mediates the rule of God to other persons or institutions, nor does any person or institution mediate the loyalty of other persons or institutions to God. The characteristic of immediacy indicates particularly the direct assertion and acknowledgment of the rulership of God in the hearts of individuals. It functions, according to Niebuhr, as the "motive" of the Protestant movement.

The nearness of the kingdom of God functions as the "goal" of the Protestant movement. The kingdom is spoken of as present reality in its primacy and immediacy. Nevertheless, in the sense of being a fully realized reality in the actual lives of individuals and workings of institutions, the kingdom is "not yet." The nearness of the kingdom speaks to the "not yetness," and at the same time raises impatient expectation. It functions not only as goal in the sense of that which is looked forward to, but that which is actively pursued. "So for Protestants the sense of catastrophe and newness of life gave urgency to the idea of the kingdom of God; it was necessary to press into it."[5]

The kingdom of God is thus presented by Niebuhr as a dynamic principle. It is a rulership being exercised; it is a kingdom being brought into being. The churches are called to be loyal to this kingdom. Loyalty also is dynamic. It includes announcing the reality of the kingdom, demonstrating obedience to it, and pressing into it. "The kingdom of God is at hand," is announcement, declaration of allegiance, and call to action.

America, writes Niebuhr, offered a unique opportunity for constructive application of the principle of the kingdom of God.

> Here Protestantism could turn from protest and conflict to construction. It not only could but needed to do so, for while there was no royal or Roman Church here against which to raise protest neither was there any church at all. If there was no Stuart monarchy here to interfere with loyalty to the divine sovereign and his laws, save in the distance, neither was there government of any sort. There were no settled institutions defending the special privileges of the religiously, politically or economically powerful; but by the same token there were no social organizations of any kind to provide for orderly procedure in the contact of men with men.[6]

In applying the theme of the kingdom of God to the American experience Niebuhr links each of the three characteristics with a particular articulation. When its primacy (center) is being stressed, the kingdom is articulated as the "sovereignty of God"; when its immediacy (motive) is being stressed, it is articulated as the "reign of Christ"; and when its nearness (goal) is being stressed, it is articulated as the "kingdom on earth." He sees all three of these articulations running throughout the history of Protestantism in America, but each particular period in history is dominated by one of them.

In the 17th century the emphasis was on the existing sovereignty of God. For the Puritans loyalty to the kingdom of God and "obedience to its laws were the conditions of their temporal and eternal welfare."[7] The problem was not to establish the rulership of God but to incorporate that rule already established from eternity, into the institutional foundations of the new nation.

The reign of Christ, as the dominant aspect of the kingdom of God in the 18th century, emphasized the coming of the kingdom immediately to the individual. If there were to be obedience to the rulership of God, individuals must be freed from their obedience to other rulerships. The individual is set at liberty through the personal receiving of the ministry of Christ, and consequent releasing of the God-serving intentions and energies.

There is the expectation that this new beginning will be expressed in obedience and works of love on the part of those within whom Christ reigns. Thus God's rulership is expressed in the life of the nation through loving care for the "least of the brethren." If a symbol for 17th century Protestantism might be the Puritan commonwealth, that of 18th century Protestantism might be the frontier revival and its off-spring, the voluntary service association.

Niebuhr suggests that the 19th century articulation of the kingdom on earth is a logical development of the kingdom idea. When the kingdom has taken root in individual lives, there follows the expectation of the kingdom taking root in the institutional life of society. If God truly is sovereign, then his sovereignty must be visible throughout life. The symbol of this emphasis might be the anti-slavery movement within the churches. For the kingdom truly to come on earth, not only must the bruises of the slaves be tended by loving individuals, but the system of slavery itself must be abolished. Changed hearts should lead to a changed social order.

Each of these articulations of loyalty to the kingdom of God has been subject to deterioration and perversions. The kingdom as the sovereignty of God deteriorates into the sovereignty of the nation, where one nation claims to be the embodiment and bearer of God's sovereignty. Tyranny in domestic affairs and imperialism in international affairs are logical outcomes of such a perversion. The kingdom as the reign of Christ deteriorates into an emotionalism which overlooks the need for thought and action, and into individualism which neglects the communal dimensions of loyalty. Finally, loyalty as the kingdom on earth deteriorates into a legitimating of the status quo as the kingdom having come in its fullness, losing the sense of crisis, of urgency which accompanies the authentic expression of the kingdom in the "not yetness" of its coming.

Jerald Brauer's <u>Protestantism in America</u>, brings the story of the churches into the 20th century.[8] Several relevant observations about the contemporary churches may be made on the basis of that source. One observation is that while the emphasis in the 19th century moved toward the primacy of man's good will and deeds in the progress of the kingdom, in the 20th century there is a return to the emphasis on the "sovereignty of God," the primacy of the creative and redemptive action, to which man responds "in trust and obedience."[9]

Another observation is that ". . . American Protestantism in the late 1940's and the 1950's witnessed a resurgence of the mass revival meetings."[10] Thus, in the emphasis on committing oneself to Christ, there is also the renewal of the articulation of the kingdom as the "reign of Christ." On the other hand, Brauer notes that "somehow the appeal did not appear as great . . ." as in earlier revival movements.[11]

This points toward a third observation, i.e., the necessity of giving attention to the institutional life of society, "the kingdom on earth." So Brauer writes, in reference to the churches' involvement in "power politics":

> . . . the experimentation that marked early Protestantism continues at a higher level and in radically new forms. . . . The Protestant Churches realize that they cannot go on ministering in the same old way if they wish to be responsible to their heritage and to contemporary life.[12]

Events of the 20th century, the wars, depressions, deterioration and dissent, have interrupted the progressive approach of the kingdom on earth. Accordingly, the churches have moved to recall the people to renewed attention to the center and motive for loyalty to the kingdom. Yet the more recent developments in the churches, both as documented by Brauer and as observed first hand, indicate that the renewal of the two earlier articulations of the kingdom does not mean that the third, the kingdom as "the kingdom on earth," has been abandoned. The goal of loyalty to the kingdom is also held out, and we are encouraged to look for an intensification of efforts to discern and to move toward that goal, within the context of the other two emphases.

Loyalty to the kingdom of God requires and has informed the concern and participation of the churches in the conditions and needs of society. The manifestations of this concern and participation in history can be explained in part then by the theological principle. On the other hand it is the specific conditions and needs of society which account for the specific articulation of the kingdom in given times and places. To answer the question, "What should the churches be doing in relation to society at a given time and place?" it is necessary to look both to the theological commitment and to the social situation. For the ministers, as the professional leaders of the churches, this necessitates a concern for the general society and a sensitivity to the needs and conditions of their particular social situations.

How does our analysis of the contemporary social situation correspond to the theme of the kingdom of God and loyalty to it? Urbanization as change affirms the dynamic nature of the kingdom as the rulership of God being exercised, being brought into being. Urbanization as the agency of man reflects the participatory nature of loyalty to the kingdom. Loyalty requires of those who are loyal that they actively press into the kingdom. Urbanization as it influences the general well-being of man necessitates the ongoing concern for the kingdom's coming in the conditions and structure of society.

Thus urbanization relates to the theme of loyalty to the kingdom of God by reflecting both the presence and not-yetness of the kingdom, both the primacy of God's creative rulership and the called-for response on the part of the churches. This is perhaps to say no more than that we would expect the general stance of the churches and their leadership toward the social situation to be one of "restless affirmation": "This is the kind of situation we are led to expect; therefore we can affirm it, but we cannot be at ease in it. There is much to be done."

We previously proposed a direction for that which is to be done, from a sociological perspective, i.e., the concept of the "self-transforming society," with its required functions of sensitizing, politicizing, and legitimation. It can be shown that as the three articulations of loyalty to the kingdom have been emphasized, the churches have participated in all three of these functions. For example, the churches pointed out the possibilities in the New World for structuring the rulership of God into national life (the politicizing function). They have been concerned with providing the experiences that would motivate people to conscientious participation in society as good citizens and good neighbors (the legitimating function). The churches have also pointed out where conditions and structures needed changing for the betterment of human well-being (the sensitizing function).

The American experience thus suggests that there are points of contact between loyalty to the kingdom of God and the self-transforming society. In fact it can be said that when the churches actually have been loyal, they have been concerned with transforming society. And furthermore, the implementation of loyalty has led the churches to fulfill functions similar to those necessary for the self-transforming society.

Nevertheless, while all three functions have been fulfilled in some way by the churches in the American experience, their predominant function for society appears to have been that of legitimation. Berger and Luckmann suggest that this is the case in their Social Construction of Reality. They point out that the churches typically provide that universe of meaning which supports the social process, making it worthy of participation.[13] Society then reciprocally affirms the legitimacy of the churches, tending to lock them into support of the given situation. That this has been especially true in the American experience is the thesis of Sidney Mead's The Lively Experiment.

The "lively experiment" is the free church system, and in this system ". . . the work of these free churches is the foundation for 'order in government and obedience to laws.' The churches thus make their necessary contribution to the 'public welfare.'"[14] The outcome of this arrangement, Mead contends, is in effect a "religious endorsement of a particular way of life," the American Way, and as complete an identification of the churches ". . . with nationalism and their country's political and economic systems as had ever been known in Christendom."[15]

The American experience includes the expectation that legitimation will be the normative mode of the churches' participation in society as a whole. The American arrangement of disestablished churches gives structural support to this expectation. It makes legitimation to the churches' own self-interest; and it makes the general public more accessible to the churches than are the decision-makers and implementers, or the decision-making and implementing processes.

But legitimation, uncritically provided, is neither consistent with loyalty to the kingdom nor functional to the self-transforming society. To be consistent with loyalty to the kingdom, uncritical legitimation assumes that the social process and organization reflect affirmation of the sovereignty of God alone and pursuit of the well-being of his children. It is this assumption that underlay the churches' initial endorsement of the American social arrangement and direction, including the free church "experiment." To be functional to the self-transforming society, uncritical legitimation assumes that the sensitizing and politicizing functions are being fulfilled. Our analysis indicates that the politicizing function is not being adequately fulfilled, either in its sensitivity to the full range of needs and opportunities for policy-formation and implementation or in its concern for the general well-being of the public.

This suggests that loyalty to the kingdom in a situation characterized by urbanization requires participation in the sensitizing and politicizing functions if the legitimating function is to be sustained. And while our analysis of the theological commitment of the churches and the American experience shows that those functions can be validly fulfilled by the churches, it also indicates that they may be difficult to fulfill. Brauer's comment about "radically new forms" and participation in the "power politics of the big city" suggests that the churches are indeed moving toward these forms of participation. Much of the contemporary discussion of the conduct of the churches, both within and without the churches themselves, provides further evidence of such participation and of the difficulty involved.

If the churches do not pursue the task of loyalty to the kingdom in ways appropriate to the societal situation, we would anticipate that ministers would be engaged almost exclusively in the legitimating function. They would construe their responsibility as ministers to be to develop and encourage faithful individual participation of the members of the church in society. They would do this by supporting the validity of socially acceptable roles and by ministering to the needs of those for whom the demands of these roles are too great.

This suggests a largely pastoral and priestly conception of social participation, carried out almost exclusively within the church's own institutional structures. It would be a parochial style of social participation.

On the other hand, if the churches and their ministers do pursue the task of loyalty to the kingdom in ways appropriate to the societal situation, we would anticipate that the ministers would be involved in the sensitizing and politicizing functions as a pre-condition for fulfilling the legitimating function. Involvement in these concerns would call for the minister's critical assessment of the given social process and organization. He would want to know if the society's official acknowledgement of the sovereignty of God and concern for the well-being of all the people is reflected in the actual workings and consequences of society.

We would expect the ministers to be engaged in social analysis and evaluation, and in communicating their conclusions to policy-makers and implementers through sermons, articles, and conversations with public officials, as well as public testifying. Beyond this the minister would also be expected to engage in the actual policy formation and implementing process by taking and supporting specific policy stands, running for political office, and organizing and participating in para-political structures. This would be a public style of social participation.

## SUMMARY

On the basis of the sociological and theological background, we would expect to see and would want to see the public style in contemporary parish ministry. As a hypothesis that can be explored through empirical research, we propose that:

> The public style is a dimension of the practice of the Protestant parish ministry that can be observed in the ministers' social participation.

We also propose two qualifying specifications of this hypothesis:

> The public style tends to be more observable the more the specific parish area is affected by those conditions of change which produce the outward appearance and inner sense of lack of public control of change;
>
> Within specific communities there are variations in the social participation of the ministers which can be accounted for in terms of denominational affiliation within Protestantism.

The framework thus provided can be sharpened further by considering it in terms of a particular context of society and its churches. This in turn will complete the groundwork for our empirical investigation.

# CHAPTER II

## CONTEXT FOR PARTICIPATION

### Chicago

The metropolitan area of Chicago shows all of the typical characteristics of urbanization. In population, the metropolitan area is growing, but the city itself has leveled off. The proportion of the non-white population rises rapidly in the city, but scarcely at all in the surrounding suburbs.

Housing is getting older in the city where new housing is made possible only by tearing down the old. In the suburbs, however, new housing can be built on previously undeveloped land. The economic situation is one of great contrasts, both within the city and between the city and suburbs. A composite economic ranking of communities (including average value of homes, assessed real estate valuation per person, and family income) illustrates the city-suburban contrast. Among the 50 highest ranking are 11 city community areas (13 percent of the total community areas), and 39 suburbs (23.5 percent of the total suburbs). Among the 50 lowest rankings, 42 are city community areas (50 percent of the total community areas), and 8 are suburbs (4.8 percent of the total suburbs).[1]

There are both predominantly white and non-white communities among the lower rankings, but the non-white communities as a whole (including several suburbs) tend to be concentrated in these lower rankings. Chicago is indeed an urban area in its changing demographic characteristics. But the change differs according to whether one is referring to the city or the suburbs, the white or the non-white populations.

The style of life in this urban area includes the urbane life of affluence: interest in entertainment and culture, modernity, adult associations, and mobility. Nevertheless, the urbane style is hardly dominant in Chicago. Much of the area's life is oriented to work and home, is less than affluent, and is strong in family associations. One of the most striking evidences of a non-urbane style is the continued identity and function of local community areas within the city of Chicago.

About forty years ago 75 community areas were delineated for the purposes of social science research. At the time these 75 areas defined

> a set of subareas of the city each of which could be regarded as having a history of its own as a community, a name, an awareness on the part of its inhabitants of common interests, and a set of local businesses and organizations.[2]

Over time there has been some change in boundaries, and some eroding of community consciousness. Yet statistics continue to be gathered and organized on the basis of these areas (with some division into A and B parts) and "they remain, in many cases, meaningful local communities."[3]

Further evidence of this local community phenomenon in contemporary Chicago is the presence of numerous community-membership organizations, home-owner associations and block clubs. The feeling of neighborhood described in the following excerpts from a civic club speech is not mere nostalgia or public relations rhetoric:

> One of the unique characteristics of Chicago is that its neighborhoods seem to have real senses of their own existence. These neighborhoods are not merely people who happen to sleep in the same areas; instead, they have a real sense of place and community. As a result, they work together to establish and maintain the citizen participation so vital to the health of any city.
>
> . . . . . . . . . . . . . . . . . . . . . . . . . . . . . . . .
>
> With all of her gussied-up svelte new look, Chicago, I think, is still a nice Midwest matron, eager to make friends with the new folks down the block. Even if it is a big city, Chicago is--well, neighborly.[4]

The concentration and extension of decision-making and implementation in urban centers of communication, finance, and government is evident in Chicago's Central Business District, "the Loop." In the kind of information the people of Chicago receive, the products that are available for purchase, the prices they pay, and employment opportunities that are open, the Loop exercises significant control over their lives. Yet there is probably little awareness of this control since its impact is delivered through persons and agencies far removed from the decision-makers themselves.

The people of Chicago are most aware of the political control which is centered in City Hall and the person of Mayor Richard J. Daley. City Hall and Mayor Daley are perceived as the point of ultimate control of Chicago's services: quality of public education; the regularity of garbage pickup; the integrity of the police department; the consistency of building code enforcement; the distribution of public housing sites; and the maintenance of public parks.

The popular perception of Daley's power appears to be well-grounded. He has been chairman of the Central Democratic Committee of Cook County since 1953 and Mayor of the City of Chicago since 1955. These offices give him power in state and national politics as well.

The link between Daley and the people is the regular Democratic ward organization, in which the precinct captain is the key person.

> The efficient precinct captain . . . knows every person in his precinct, he helps move in the newcomers, assists the living, buries the dead. He is, in short, the closest person a voter has to his government. If he does his job well, he will be rewarded in turn by the voter casting his ballot as the precinct captain suggests. Not uncommonly as poll-takers

> visit these areas asking voter intent, the answer they get is: "The way my precinct captain says." This is the quid pro quo of politics.[5]

The concentration of political power and control in Chicago also provides a structure for lines of communication and responsibility to and from the people. There is serious questioning as to how well the system works, however.

The agency of man as the producer of change is also evident in Chicago. In 1909, Daniel H. Burnham and Edward H. Bennett produced for Chicago one of the first comprehensive city plans on this continent. Chicago is the birthplace of the skyscraper, and continues to be a leader in "vertical architecture." Structurally the city is in a constant state of being built and rebuilt. Its freeways, subways, elevated network, and airports are the product of man's ingenuity in transportation.

Of course other less attractive aspects of the city--crime, air and water pollution, deterioration, segregated housing, and much of its disease and injury--are also a result of man's agency. But whether it is praise for what has gone right, or blame for what has gone wrong, it is man's agency that is acknowledged. Chicago has had its share of those who leave for other parts when situations get too bad, but it also has a tradition of fighting back through ingenuity, planning, and organization.

There have already been a number of indications that urbanization has not made a totally positive contribution to the well-being of those who live in Chicago. There are three kinds of changes in which the need for control is evident. The first are those which affect the area generally: the aging of communities, the pollution of air and water, the rising cost of city administration, and the block by block expansion of segregated black residential areas are examples. These changes affect the whole metropolitan area. They add misery to the lives of those who stay; they make it more and more expensive and inconvenient to escape the misery and still retain access to the city's employment, shopping, and cultural opportunities.

In the second group are changes that are planned but do not take into consideration the general well-being of the people as the public. The condemnation of residential neighborhoods for the construction of shopping centers and the conversion of open land to highways and real estate development are examples. In these changes the public good is often invoked as the motivation, but private interests of power and profit seem to be the chief beneficiaries.

In the third group are changes which to some extent affect people throughout the metropolitan area, but which seem to be more prevalent in some areas than in others. Increasing incidence of crime, unemployment, substandard and crowded housing, disease and dirt are examples of such changes.

There are, for example, 15 community areas in the city of Chicago where the chances of residents living in substandard housing range from 22 out of 100 to 68 out of 100; on the other hand, there are 15 community areas where the chances are less than 1¼ out of 100.

It is significant to note the concentration of the poor housing, unemployment, and disease in the sections of the city extending from the Loop southward and westward. Furthermore, according to a 1966 population study, the percentage of non-white population in these areas ranges from 37.6 to 99.1 (only one being less than 60 percent). On the other hand, the "good" areas are in the far northwest or far southwest sections of the city. The percentage of their non-white populations ranges from 0.0 to 7.6 (only one having more than 0.2 percent).[6]

One would expect to find evidence of concern for controlling the forces of urbanization for the well-being of the general public throughout the Chicago area. But, one would expect this concern to be more apparent in some areas than in others.

This concern is indeed present and is being organized. Much of the organizing is taking place outside of the regular Democratic ward organization, indicating that that organization is not satisfactorily linking the public with the mayoral center of power. Some of the organization is within the formal political system. The increasing number of Republican candidates for office, especially within the black communities, as well as Democratic candidates running independently of the Daley organization, are evidence of this.

In addition there has been a significant amount of civil rights-oriented organization. The Southern Christian Leadership Conference and the Congress on Racial Equality have been active in Chicago. The Coordinating Council of Community Organizations is an attempt to coordinate all of the efforts to bring racial equality to the city.

One of the most vital manifestations of organization for control is the network of community membership organizations, which includes almost every block of the city. These are sometimes categorized as para-political organizations, political in nature, yet operating parallel to the formal political organization. These community organizations vary widely in their attitudes toward change. All of them, however, are attempts to organize those who live or have businesses in a geographically delineated area, in order to bring under control the forces that contribute to the community's being a better or worse place in which to live and do business. The Woodlawn Organization, the Lincoln Park Homeowners Association, and the West Avalon Community Organization are examples of this kind of organization.

In terms of the functions of a self-transforming society, the politicizing function appears to be dominant in Chicago, particularly in the city itself. In Chicago, the way to get things done is through political action--decision-making and power-mobilization. Richard Daley's administration encourages working through City Hall. The new organizations are more apt to operate against City Hall. They acknowledge that City Hall can get things done, but organized pressure must be brought to bear upon it. Or they work in place of City Hall, under the assumption that if something is going to be done in the community, the community itself will have to do it.

The success of non-City Hall organization indicates both the need for social transformation, and City Hall's unsatisfactory fulfilling of the necessary functions. Two alternatives present themselves. The first is to open up the sensitizing and legitimating functions now serving the politicizing function of City Hall, the better to include and serve the public. The second is to organize parallel politicizing functions in which the sensitizing and legitimating functions are more open to the local communities, or the community as a whole. The parallel political function can be exercised either directly, by doing the things that need doing, or indirectly, by pressuring City Hall to do them. The alternatives are not mutually exclusive.

## Chicago's Churches

In the introduction to a volume describing the "new forms of the church in Chicago," one writer has stated, "In the past few years, Chicago has become the focal point of invigorating innovation in American church life."[7]

This is an evaluative comment on the churches of Chicago. What are some of the underlying facts? One can begin with broad statements about church membership. The Chicago Archdiocese (Cook and Lake Counties) is the country's most populous Roman Catholic Diocese, and the Chicago-Midwest Region has the largest concentration of Protestants in the nation. The Archdiocese reports a membership of 2,318,000 (including children) in 1964, and the 19 Protestant denominations for whom statistics are available report 533,022 members (excluding children under thirteen years of age) for the same area in 1963. Obviously the Roman Catholic membership is much larger than that of the combined Protestant membership. To give added perspective to Protestant strength, their city membership of 250,787 is but 9.2 percent of the total population. The suburban Cook County membership is a somewhat higher 15.9 percent of the total suburban white population.[8]

Excluded from these figures are the major black denominations for which published data were not available. A 1965 survey, however, indicates that these denominations are the largest Protestant groups in the city of Chicago. Table 1 gives membership statistics for the city's eight largest Protestant denominations, with a parallel column showing the memberships of the same groups in the total Cook, Lake, DuPage, and Will counties area.

The churches are also present through their institutions. In addition to the hundreds of congregations, practically all with their own buildings for worship, there are 24 graduate schools of theology and major seminaries, and 12 undergraduate and minor seminaries. There are 23 church-related colleges and universities, 6 Bible training schools, and 700 parochial grade schools, high schools and academies. In addition there are 200 welfare and other social service agencies including hospitals, homes for children and the aged, and settlement and neighborhood houses.

TABLE 1

PROTESTANT CHURCH MEMBERSHIP, 1965

| Denomination | City, Number of Members[a] | Four Counties, Number of Members[b] |
|---|---|---|
| National Baptist Convention, Inc. | [95,000][c] | 95,000 |
| National Baptist Convention | [68,200][c] | 68,200 |
| Lutheran Church-Missouri Synod | 43,788 | 112,578 |
| Lutheran Church in America | 37,000 | 72,434 |
| Methodist Church | 34,713 | 125,007 |
| United Church of Christ | 34,000 | 95,769 |
| United Presbyterian Church | 29,218 | 84,423 |
| Episcopal Church | 13,033 | 42,760 |

[a]Bureau of Research, Research Report No. 2-1167, Table CFGC-8.

[b]Bureau of Research, "Research Memo," Church Federation of Greater Chicago, August, 1965, p. 1. (Mimeographed.)

[c]While data are given only for the four counties, it is assumed that membership in this denomination is almost exclusively in city congregations.

The many regional and national denominational headquarters in Chicago provide special leadership resources as well as positions of power for Chicago churches. The Archdiocese of Chicago, the Rock River Conference of the Methodist Church, and the Illinois Synod of the Lutheran Church in America have their headquarters in Chicago. The national offices of the Evangelical Covenant Church and several agencies of the Lutheran Church in America and the Lutheran Council-USA are also located there.

It would seem valid to observe that these forms of the churches' presence lend themselves most effectively to articulation of the kingdom as the "reign of Christ," giving attention to the "motive" for loyalty to the kingdom. Motivation is promoted through the efforts of individual congregations, centered around membership recruitment and education. The welfare and social service agencies then can provide the structures through which well-motivated members can serve their individual fellow-men in need. This also provides encouragement and structure for a parochial style of the ministers' participation in the community.

The churches are present in other forms, however. The Church Federation of Greater Chicago, the Chicago Conference on Religion and Race, and the National Conference of Christians and Jews are cooperative ventures which have moved into new program areas. The churches are present in consciously innovative form in the Urban Training Center for Christian Mission and the Ecumenical Institute, both of which train leadership with specific reference to the urbanization of society. The Community Renewal Society specializes in innovating church forms with the expectation that they will be taken over by the traditional forms of the church. The Archdiocese has its aggressive Office of Urban Affairs.

In addition there are numerous cooperative groupings of local congregations such as the North Side Cooperative Ministry, the Christian Action Mission, and the Northwest Lutheran Parish. Some of the concerns of these cooperative efforts are parochial in nature, but there is a significant public dimension to them as well. The churches identify with the community at large in their participation in community membership organizations. The Interreligious Council on Urban Affairs is organized specifically for mobilizing funds and technical assistance for such community organizations.

In these activities the other two dimensions of loyalty to the kingdom of God are more likely to be present. To the extent that they are conscious attempts publicly to voice the claims of God upon the life of the metropolitan area, they pursue the kingdom as the "sovereignty of God," recalling the community to the "center of loyalty." To the extent that they are conscious efforts to organize and shape the life of the community, they pursue the kingdom as the "kingdom on earth." And they can provide encouragement and structure for a public style of community participation.

The residential congregation, being the primary operational base of the ministers, is crucial for our study. The continued identity and functioning of the Chicago neighborhoods is accompanied by the continued identity and functioning of neighborhood congregations as the predominant form of the church. In itself this would seem to facilitate the parochial style of participation. Yet the local community is where organization for public control of change is centered, which could encourage a public style of participation. Thus the local congregation may serve both to hinder and facilitate the public style of social participation.

In summary, this over-view of Chicago has demonstrated those conditions in both society and church which led us to expect a public style of participation of ministers in their communities. It is possible and helpful at this point to propose further qualifications of this expectation, in terms of the specific Chicago situation.

1. The public style should be more observable in the ministry of those pastors whose parishes are located in the areas extending south and west from the center of the city, and in the adjacent areas, and less observable in the areas farthest out from the center and in the suburban areas.

2. Because of the relatively small size of the white Protestant membership in the Chicago area, we would expect considerable cooperation not only among white Protestant ministers, but between them and black Protestant ministers and Roman Catholic priests, as well as general community persons and agencies.

3. We would expect that the ministers' participation in their communities would center either in opening up the legitimating and sensitizing functions serving the formal politicizing function, or in para-politicizing functions with their accompanying sensitizing and legitimating functions. Another alternative would be participating in competing formal politicizing functions, e.g., through Republican or Independent Democratic organizations.

## Design for Research[9]

To provide empirical data for this study, the survey method of research was employed. We asked the persons in whose roles we were interested to describe and interpret their own actions. In addition to producing appropriate data, the survey method allowed for a fairly broad sampling with limited resources.

After delineating the metropolitan area which was to serve as the sample, the Chicago Community Areas and the suburban municipalities were designated as the sampling units. These units were then sorted into three groups of incidence of human welfare needs: "high," "medium," and "low." As indices we used categories defined by the Welfare Council of Metropolitan Chicago: family income under $3,000, male unemployment, substandard housing, juvenile delinquency, individuals receiving public assistance, new cases of tuberculosis, and illegitimacy.[10] The "high" and "low" units are at the extremes of the distribution--very high incidence of human welfare needs, or very low. Since exactly equivalent data for the suburban units were not available to us, the newer, higher social rank suburbs[11] were selected and included in the "low" category.

After stratifying the community units the survey sample was selected. We had a rough idea of the number of ministers and therefore the number of communities that we could cover with the survey. There were certain communities which we wanted to include because of the marked presence or absence of organized response to community problems. In addition we wanted to have a good denominational cross-section within the areas to control for that factor. On the basis of these criteria six "high," nine "middle," and five "low" community units were selected as the survey sample. The units are listed in Table 2 and are located geographically in Figure 1.

In three cases adjacent community areas with similar rankings have been combined to form one unit, in order to get the proper representation of churches. Of the "high" units all but West Town have predominantly black populations, and in the "middle" units Greater Grand Crossing and

TABLE 2

SURVEY SAMPLE, COMMUNITIES

| Name of Community | Percentage, Non-White Population, 1966[a] |
|---|---|
| "High" Incidence Communities[b] | |
| West Town | 2.4 |
| North Lawndale | 94.6 |
| Englewood | 82.6 |
| Washington Park-Grand Blvd. | 99.0 and 99.1 |
| Woodlawn | 98.3 |
| East-West Garfield Park | 87.5 and 68.7 |
| "Middle" Incidence Communities | |
| Greater Grand Crossing | 96.9 |
| Chatham-Avalon Park | 88.0 and 25.6 |
| Uptown | 4.8 |
| Humboldt Park | 2.9 |
| Lincoln Park | 7.5 |
| Roseland | 24.9 |
| Austin | 0.6 |
| Auburn Gresham | 34.7 |
| Bridgeport | 0.4 |
| "Low" Incidence Communities | |
| Beverly | 0.1 |
| West Ridge | 0.2 |
| South Holland | 0.1 |
| Westchester | 0.0 |
| Skokie | 0.3 |

[a] Study by Hospital Planning Council for Metropolitan Chicago, reported in, Chicago Sun-Times, January 13, 1967, p. 4.

[b] In a newspaper article subsequent to the sample selection, all of these communities, except Washington Park, were listed as "sensitive spots," ". . . areas of Chicago that poverty and experience make more vulnerable than others [to summer violence]." Chicago Sun-Times, June 4, 1967, p. 1.

Fig. 1.--Survey Sample, Communities

Key[a]

2--West Ridge
3--Uptown
7--Lincoln Park
23--Humboldt Park
24--West Town
25--Austin
26, 27--East, West Garfield Park
29--North Lawndale
38, 40--Grand Blvd., Washington Park
42--Woodlawn
44, 45--Chatham, Avalon Park
49--Roseland
60--Bridgeport
68--Englewood
69--Greater Grand Crossing
71--Auburn Gresham
72--Beverly
A--Skokie
B--Westchester
C--South Holland

[a]Numbers correspond to those used in designating Chicago local community areas in Kitagawa and Taeuber, Local Community Fact Book.

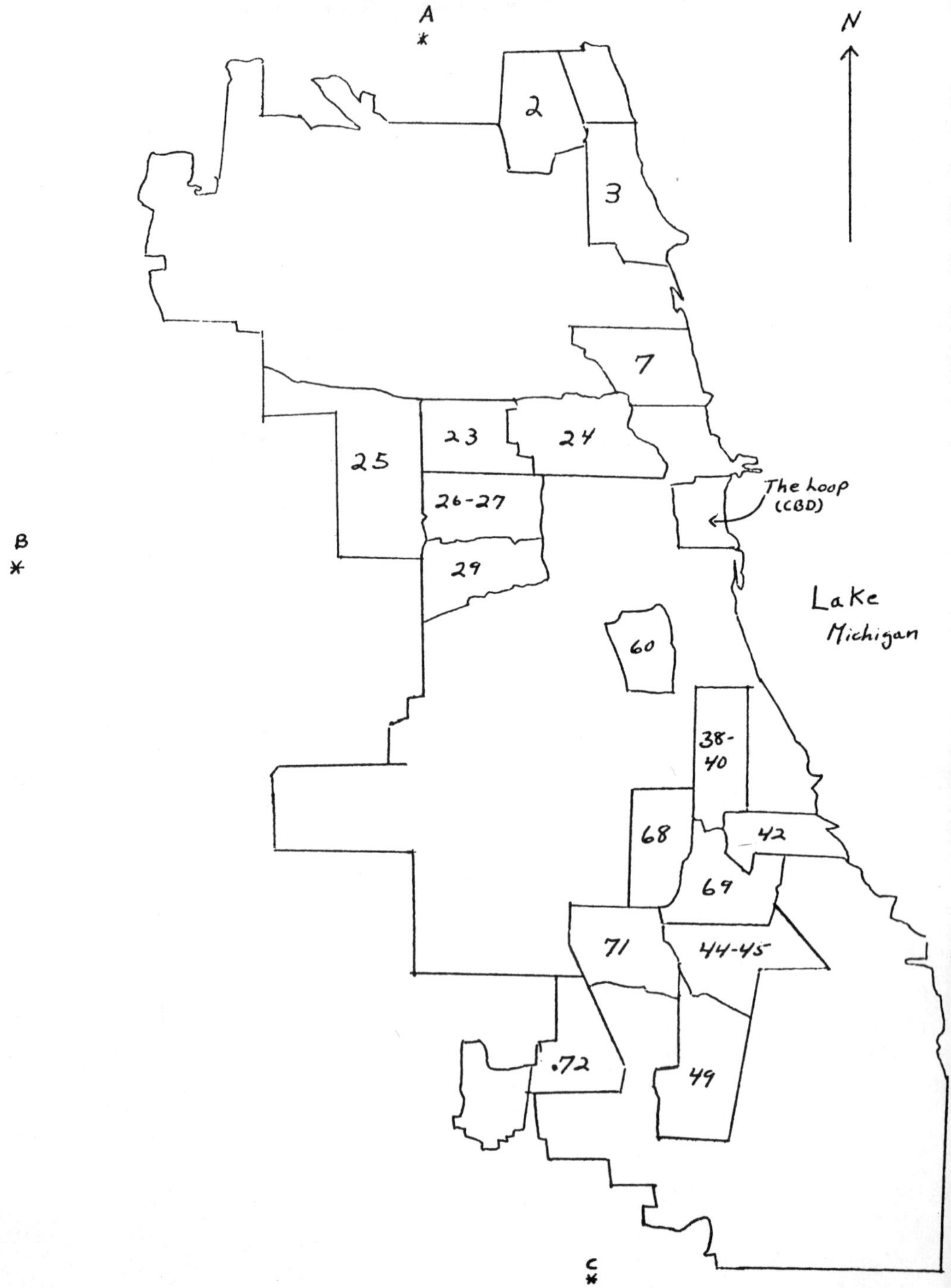
A
N
2
3
7
23
24
25
26-27
29
The Loop
(CBD)
B
Lake
Michigan
60
38-
40
68
42
69
71
44-45
72
49
C

Chatham-Avalon Park have predominantly black populations. The remaining units in the "middle" category as well as the "low" areas are predominantly or almost exclusively white in population.

The sample of ministers was limited to denominations which have congregational representation in almost all the community units: Episcopal; Lutheran Church in America; Lutheran Church-Missouri Synod; Methodist; United Presbyterian; United Church of Christ. These are the six denominations named earlier as the largest predominantly white Protestant groups in the Chicago area.

All of the ministers of congregations of these six denominations within the community unit sample were included in the primary ministerial sample. The total primary sample thus drawn is 138, distributed as noted in Table 3. The sample includes the ministers of roughly one-fourth of the congregations of the six denominations in the metropolitan area.

TABLE 3

SURVEY SAMPLE, DENOMINATIONAL REPRESENTATION

| Denomination | Number of Congregations |
|---|---|
| Episcopal | 16 |
| Lutheran Church in America | 23 |
| Lutheran Church-Missouri Synod | 25 |
| Methodist | 31 |
| United Presbyterian | 21 |
| United Church of Christ | 22 |
| Total | 138 |

Two instruments for gathering data were used.[12] The first is a pre-coded, forced-response questionnaire, which provides data on a number of items which can easily be reduced to a fixed number of alternative answers: items about the congregation, the community, the minister himself and his ministry in relation to the community; evaluation of certain community agencies and statements of theological and sociological orientation on Likert-type scales.

The second instrument is a structured, open-response interview schedule. The schedule sets the agenda for the minister's response; the minister decides the content of the agenda items. For example, the schedule asks for response in terms of the most urgent community problem, community response to the problems, and the minister's own response; the specific topics he talks about are open within those broad categories. Other items in the interview are the response of the congregation to the minister's community activity, his relation to other community ministers and to his own denomination in this area of his ministry, and the theological grounding of his activity.

### Summary

Chapter I provided the theoretical framework for the research. Chapter II has given the concrete setting and methodology for the research. It is within the overall orientation provided by these two chapters that the following chapters should be considered.

# CHAPTER III

## PATTERNS OF PARTICIPATION

In this chapter, we describe the Chicago ministers statistically, both as a single group, and broken down into sub-groups. The purpose is to determine what patterns in style of community participation may be present among them. In the subsequent chapter, we attempt to retrieve something of the individuality of the ministers by considering a number of them as particular persons functioning in specific communities.

### The Sample as a Whole

The description of the Chicago ministers, considered as a single group, can be quickly given. To begin with the following seems to be true of most of the ministers, according to our survey.[1]

They are aware of the communities in which they minister to the extent of being able to name them, to assess their problems and to evaluate them as places to live. (Q, 14, 15, 16)[2] In their evaluation of society in general, they give only qualified endorsement to things as they are and tend to disagree with a number of established societal values, e.g., faith in "the American Way," and reliance on the "judgments of experts." (Q, 19)

In their preaching and teaching most ministers give some consideration to the problems of their communities and the necessity for congregational member response. (Q, 26) Furthermore, most ministers have themselves taken some concrete action in response to the community situation, in addition to preaching and teaching. (Q, 32)

Additional observations must be qualified by the larger or smaller percentages of ministers to whom they apply. In terms of the degree or priority of their community participation, 36 percent of the ministers spend less than one-tenth of their time in community activity, while 19 percent spend more than one-third of their time in this way. (I, 11) Community activity is given first or second priority in time spent by 23 percent of the ministers, while 43 percent give it fourth priority (relative to three other aspects of their ministry: preaching, teaching, public worship; pastoral calling and counseling; administrative work. (Q, 25)

In identifying the problems of the community, approximately equal numbers of ministers name lack of community responsibility, inadequate community representation, inappropriate community attitudes toward other ethnic groups and poor community conditions, as the most urgent problem. (I, 1, 2) About one-third of the ministers consider the basic cause of community problems to be the new social situation generally; a like proportion cite the unequal distribution of power, and about one-fifth each the lack of responsibility, and the fears and prejudices of the residents. (I, 3)

The ministers' evaluation of various strategies or organizations attempting to deal with community problems ranges from 70 percent favoring the moderate approach of the Church Federation, to 53 percent the more militant approach of the Woodlawn Organization, to about 20 percent favoring both the conventional approach of the Billy Graham Crusade and the militant Student Nonviolent Coordinating Committee. (Q, 18) In their evaluation of the effectiveness of agencies working locally, about one-third consider none at all to be effective, and another one-third consider the local community membership organization to be most effective, while 5 percent consider their own congregation to be most effective. (I, 5)

As to their own participation, almost nine out of ten of the ministers took some kind of action directed toward the community through their own congregational programs, but only about six out of ten through some kind of non-congregational "parapolitical" activity. (Q, 32) About four out of ten of the ministers participated in a local community organization, but three out of ten participated in no community membership association at all. (Q, 33) While, as noted above, only 5 percent of the ministers considered their own congregation to be the most effective agency, about 40 percent of them specify their own congregation as that agency through which they participate most actively in community matters. The remaining 60 percent participate most actively through non-congregational agencies. (I, 7)

The agency's adequacy in representing the needs and desires of the community is the paramount consideration for participation for about three-fourths of the ministers, while for one-fourth it is the agency's ability actually to accomplish its objectives. The agency's consideration of interests beyond those of its immediate community is a criterion for about one-tenth of the ministers. (Some obviously cited more than one criterion.) (I, 7)

In their general orientation to community problems about one-fifth of the ministers see cause and needed response in terms of the qualification of individuals and communities for receiving and making use of available resources and opportunities. About two-fifths see cause and response in terms of the community's organization for presenting and pursuing its particular interests. The other two-fifths see cause and response in terms of the larger social system's structure for allocating power among the various societal units.

According to our development of the hypothesis, together with its qualifying hypotheses, the following would tend to validate the "presence" of the public style:

1. An awareness of the local community as an identifiable entity with its own problems and opportunities for living;

2. **A minimal participation in the life of the community as a part of ministry, with some movement toward making this one of the major thrusts of ministry;**

3. **Participation in programs and agencies addressing the community situation, other than those of the congregational structure;**

4. **Participation in activity which tends to fulfill the functions of sensitizing and politicizing more than that of legitimation;**

5. **Participation in politicizing activities which tend to be of a parapolitical rather than of an "established" political nature.**

**Based on the data summarized above it seems valid to conclude that the public style is present and observable in the social participation of a majority of our sample of ministers. While some aspects of this participation appear to be present throughout the sample, there are other aspects within which there is considerable variation in the degree of their presence.**

## The Local Community Factor[3]

The great majority of ministers in all three community types identify their communities either by the name used by us in our sample selection or by that of a subsection. However, as one would expect, there are sharp differences in the ranking of communities as places to live compared with other areas in Chicago. The rankings in Table 4 (Q, 16) tend to validate the sample designations, i.e., ministers in the "high" incidence communities tend to rate their communities as below average, those of "middle communities" as about average, and those of the "low" communities as above average.

TABLE 4

LOCAL COMMUNITY LIVABILITY, BY COMMUNITY TYPE

| Rating | Percentage of All Ministers | Percentage of Ministers by Type of Community: High | Middle | Low |
|---|---|---|---|---|
| Below average | 26 | 62 | 16 | 0 |
| About average | 30 | 24 | 41 | 5 |
| Above average | 36 | 7 | 32 | 90 |
| No response | 8 | 7 | 11 | 5 |
| Total | 100 | 100 | 100 | 100 |

$X^2 = 52.09$; D.F. = 4; .001 level.[a]

[a] Unless otherwise noted $x^2$ statistics do not include "no response," or "don't know, no response" rows.

Differences by community type are especially noticeable in Table 5 (Q, 15) in which the assessment of local communities in terms of particular problems is summarized.

For all problems except "racial prejudice," the highest proportion of ministers assessing them as "serious" is in the "high" communities. In all problems except "racial prejudice" and "mental, emotional stress," the highest proportion of ministers assessing them as "not a problem" is in the "low" communities. The piling up of welfare problems in the "high" communities includes "family instability" and "mental, emotional stress." They are considered "somewhat" a problem by a large proportion of the ministers of the "middle" and "low" communities, but ministers of the "high" communities report them as "serious" problems.

TABLE 5

ASSESSMENT OF LOCAL COMMUNITY PROBLEMS, BY COMMUNITY TYPE

| Community Problem | Assessment | Percentage of All Ministers | Percentage of Ministers by Type of Community | | |
|---|---|---|---|---|---|
| | | | High | Middle | Low |
| Youth gangs | Serious | 22 | 48 | 16 | 0 |
| | Somewhat | 54 | 45 | 64 | 40 |
| | No problem | 16 | 3 | 11 | 50 |
| | Don't know, no response | 8 | 4 | 9 | 10 |
| | Total | 100 | 100 | 100 | 100 |
| $x^2 = 13.38$; D.F. = 4; .01 level | | | | | |
| Deteriorating housing | Serious | 33 | 79 | 21 | 0 |
| | Somewhat | 31 | 17 | 48 | 5 |
| | No problem | 28 | 0 | 20 | 90 |
| | Don't know, no response | 8 | 4 | 11 | 5 |
| | Total | 100 | 100 | 100 | 100 |
| $x^2 = 76.24$; D.F. = 4; .001 level | | | | | |
| Inadequate public education | Serious | 38 | 69 | 36 | 0 |
| | Somewhat | 22 | 17 | 29 | 10 |
| | No problem | 30 | 7 | 23 | 85 |
| | Don't know, no response | 10 | 7 | 12 | 5 |
| | Total | 100 | 100 | 100 | 100 |
| $x^2 = 42.15$; D.F. = 4; .001 level | | | | | |

TABLE 5.--Continued

| Community Problem | Assessment | Percentage of All Ministers | Percentage of Ministers by Type of Community | | |
|---|---|---|---|---|---|
| | | | High | Middle | Low |
| Police harassment | Serious | 10 | 34 | 0 | 0 |
| | Somewhat | 15 | 28 | 13 | 5 |
| | No problem | 61 | 24 | 70 | 90 |
| | Don't know no response | 14 | 14 | 17 | 5 |
| | Total | 100 | 100 | 100 | 100 |
| $x^2 = 41.09$; D.F. = 4; .001 level | | | | | |
| Burglary, vandalism, assault | Serious | 23 | 52 | 14 | 5 |
| | Somewhat | 54 | 34 | 64 | 55 |
| | No problem | 13 | 7 | 9 | 35 |
| | Don't know, no response | 10 | 7 | 13 | 5 |
| | Total | 100 | 100 | 100 | 100 |
| $x^2 = 24.62$; D.F. = 4; .001 level | | | | | |
| Ineffective political representation | Serious | 22 | 52 | 14 | 0 |
| | Somewhat | 27 | 21 | 32 | 20 |
| | No problem | 33 | 14 | 32 | 65 |
| | Don't know no response | 18 | 13 | 22 | 15 |
| | Total | 100 | 100 | 100 | 100 |
| $x^2 = 23.97$; D.F. = 4; .001 level | | | | | |
| Racial prejudice | Serious | 38 | 38 | 39 | 35 |
| | Somewhat | 33 | 31 | 27 | 55 |
| | No problem | 16 | 14 | 23 | 0 |
| | Don't know, no response | 13 | 17 | 11 | 10 |
| | Total | 100 | 100 | 100 | 100 |
| $x^2 = 5.36$; D.F. = 4; $p > .10$ | | | | | |

TABLE 5.--Continued

| Community Problem | Assessment | Percentage of All Ministers | Percentage of Ministers by Type of Community | | |
|---|---|---|---|---|---|
| | | | High | Middle | Low |
| Family instability | Serious | 33 | 72 | 23 | 5 |
| | Somewhat | 49 | 24 | 57 | 60 |
| | No problem | 9 | 0 | 9 | 20 |
| | Don't know, no response | 9 | 4 | 11 | 15 |
| | Total | 100 | 100 | 100 | 100 |
| $x^2$ = 32.07; D.F. = 4; .001 level | | | | | |
| Mental, emotional stress | Serious | 29 | 62 | 20 | 10 |
| | Somewhat | 45 | 24 | 48 | 65 |
| | No problem | 9 | 0 | 14 | 5 |
| | Don't know, no response | 17 | 14 | 18 | 20 |
| | Total | 100 | 100 | 100 | 100 |
| $x^2$ = 22.87; D.F. = 4; .001 level | | | | | |

Effective political representation seems to be less of a problem than we had suggested in formulating the hypothesis of the public style, when the ministers are considered as a single group. In this table, however, we can see that community type makes a considerable difference. While about two-thirds of the ministers in the "low" communities see this as no problem at all, over half the ministers in the "high" communities consider it to be a "serious" problem, and almost half the ministers of the "middle" communities consider it to be at least "somewhat" a problem. The problem which is considered to be "serious" by the least proportion of the total sample (10 percent), "police harassment," is a "serious" problem to over one-third of the ministers of the "high" communities.

No matter what type of community the ministers serve in, they are aware of and are prepared to make judgments about the conditions of living in their communities. (One might question, however, whether the "low" community ministers may not be underestimating the extent to which "racial prejudice," "family instability," and "mental, emotional stress" are problems in their communities.) The type of community makes a difference in the kinds of judgments the ministers make about their communities, however.

Few ministers of any of the community types give "little" or "no" emphasis to any of the preaching and teaching subjects listed in the questionnaire. Differences related to community type do appear when we compare the ministers according to those who give "much" or "some" emphasis, as in Table 6. (Q, 26)

TABLE 6

PREACHING AND TEACHING EMPHASES, BY COMMUNITY TYPE

| Subject | Emphasis | Percentage of All Ministers | Percentage of Ministers by Type of Community: High | Middle | Low |
|---|---|---|---|---|---|
| Inner-life of faith and devotion | Much | 50 | 38 | 54 | 55 |
| | Some | 30 | 38 | 25 | 35 |
| | Little, no | 11 | 20 | 7 | 5 |
| | No response | 9 | 4 | 14 | 5 |
| | Total | 100 | 100 | 100 | 100 |
| $x^2 = 2.31$; D.F. = 2; $p > .10$ level ("much," "some" rows only). | | | | | |
| Interpersonal and family relations | Much | 40 | 52 | 38 | 30 |
| | Some | 48 | 41 | 46 | 60 |
| | Little, no | 4 | 3 | 4 | 5 |
| | No response | 8 | 4 | 12 | 5 |
| | Total | 100 | 100 | 100 | 100 |
| $x^2 = 2.48$; D.F. = 2; $p > .10$ level ("much," "some" rows only). | | | | | |
| Members' responsibility in community life | Much | 41 | 59 | 41 | 15 |
| | Some | 48 | 38 | 43 | 75 |
| | Little, no | 3 | 0 | 4 | 5 |
| | No response | 8 | 3 | 12 | 5 |
| | Total | 100 | 100 | 100 | 100 |
| $x^2 = 9.49$; D.F. = 2; .01 level ("much," "some" rows only). | | | | | |
| Large social issues of the day | Much | 36 | 59 | 29 | 25 |
| | Some | 46 | 31 | 46 | 65 |
| | Little, no | 10 | 7 | 13 | 5 |
| | No response | 8 | 3 | 12 | 5 |
| | Total | 100 | 100 | 100 | 100 |
| $x^2 = 9.14$; D.F. = 2; .02 level ("much," "some" rows only). | | | | | |

A larger proportion of ministers in the "middle" and "low" communities give "much" emphasis to the subject of the "inner-life of faith and devotion," than of the ministers of the "high" communities. On the other hand, the latter give "much" emphasis to the other subjects in greater proportion, especially in the subjects of "community life" and "social issues." This is consistent with the ministers' assessment of the seriousness of problems in their communities.

In taking public stands on particular issues, there is little difference according to community type on the issues of a "statewide open occupancy law," "air pollution control," "Negro housing protest demonstration marches in white neighborhoods," or "organized violence as a strategy for social change." On the issue of the "guaranteed annual income," however, over one-third (38 percent) of the ministers of the "high" communities have taken a stand publicly, while only one of the "low" community ministers has. About the same is true of the issue of "organizing relief recipients into welfare unions." About two-thirds of the ministers of both "high" (66 percent) and "middle" (64 percent) communities have taken a public stand on "organizing local residents for a greater voice in community decision making"; only about one-third (35 percent) of the "low" community ministers have.

Regarding the position they take when they make their public stand, ministers of all community types tend to be overwhelmingly supportive in their stands on "air pollution control," "regional planning for metropolitan development," "organizing local residents for a greater voice in community decision-making," and a "statewide open occupancy law." (The "low" community ministers' support of the latter issue takes on added significance considering the fact that 80 percent of them report their congregations to be "moderately" or "extremely opposed to open housing.") There is also overwhelming lack of support by ministers in all community types for "organized violence as a strategy for social change."

On four of the issues, however, there is some difference according to community type. As seen in Table 7, (Q, 31) ministers of the "high" communities are much more supportive of the "guaranteed annual income" and "welfare union" issues. The main difference between them and the ministers of the "low" communities is that the latter have not made a decision, rather than their being opposed in large proportion. Income maintenance and welfare matters would be of greater urgency to ministers of the "high" communities. Sensitivity to local feelings is observable in response to the other two issues also. There is less support for "neighborhood" schools by ministers whose communities would most benefit by a change in that policy and more support where change would be of questionable benefit in the minds of residents. There is also less support for the "protest marches" in those communities that tend to be disrupted by them.

There are issues where there seems to be general agreement among the ministers; where there is a difference the larger proportion of ministers take their stand with the people of their own communities. The public style corresponds in some degree then to the particular interests of the local community and especially to the urgency for these interests to be articulated.

TABLE 7

POSITION ON PUBLIC ISSUES, BY COMMUNITY TYPE

| Issue | Position | Percentage of All Ministers | Percentage of Ministers by Type of Community | | |
|---|---|---|---|---|---|
| | | | High | Middle | Low |
| Guaranteed annual income[a] | Supportive | 34 | 52 | 34 | 10 |
| | Non-supportive | 20 | 14 | 18 | 35 |
| | Undecided, no response | 46 | 34 | 48 | 55 |
| | Total | 100 | 100 | 100 | 100 |
| Organizing relief recipients into welfare unions[b] | Supportive | 30 | 55 | 25 | 10 |
| | Non-supportive | 25 | 21 | 27 | 25 |
| | Undecided, no response | 45 | 24 | 48 | 65 |
| | Total | 100 | 100 | 100 | 100 |
| Maintaining the neighborhood school policy[c] | Supportive | 36 | 24 | 43 | 35 |
| | Non-supportive | 36 | 52 | 32 | 25 |
| | Undecided, no response | 28 | 24 | 25 | 40 |
| | Total | 100 | 100 | 100 | 100 |
| Negro housing protest demonstration marches in white neighborhoods[d] | Supportive | 34 | 45 | 34 | 20 |
| | Non-supportive | 40 | 41 | 36 | 50 |
| | Undecided, no response | 26 | 14 | 30 | 30 |
| | Total | 100 | 100 | 100 | 100 |

[a] $x^2 = 7.80$; D.F. = 4; .10 level.

[b] $x^2 = 14.20$; D.F. = 4; .01 level.

[c] $x^2 = 5.18$; D.F. = 4; $p > .10$.

[d] $x^2 = 4.54$; D.F. = 4; $p > .10$.

In Table 8 (Q, 32), we see the types of action ministers take. "Congregational" action is action taken within the structure of the congregation; "public: political" is action taken primarily within the official political system; "public: parapolitical" is action taken parallel to the official political system. The percentages represent the proportion of ministers in each community type who indicated they had participated in that kind of action during the past year.

TABLE 8

ACTION PARTICIPATED IN, BY COMMUNITY TYPE

| Kind of Action | Percentage of All Ministers | Percentage of Ministers by Type of Community | | |
|---|---|---|---|---|
| | | High | Middle | Low |
| Congregational | 88 | 97 | 84 | 85 |
| Public: political | 74 | 86 | 73 | 60 |
| Public: parapolitical[a] | 57 | 72 | 57 | 35 |
| All three kinds[b] | 52 | 69 | 52 | 30 |
| None at all | 5 | 0 | 7 | 5 |
| No response | 6 | 3 | 7 | 5 |

[a]$x^2$ = 7.06; D.F. = 2; .05 level.

[b]$x^2$ = 7.41; D.F. = 2; .025 level.

The ministers of the "high" communities respond in the highest proportion in each kind of action. The most marked contrast among the three groups is in the "parapolitical" action, and in participation in all three kinds of action. It is reasonable that those who sense political representation to be most inadequate would participate most in parapolitical activity. The "middle" community ministers are in the middle in each case, but closer to the "high" community ministers in the "parapolitical" and "all three kinds" categories.

Participation in non-congregational church membership associations is about the same for ministers of all community types. Ministers of the "low" communities are active in interdenominational associations in greatest proportion (100 percent, compared to 75 percent of the "high" community ministers and 67 percent of the "middle" group). Such associations tend to focus on community issues in all types of communities.

There is greater variation in the (general) community membership associations, however, as noted in Table 9. (Q, 13) The highest proportion of "low" community minister participation is in "conventional civic" types of associations; the highest for the other two groups is the local community organization type. The latter type is not present in most of our "low" communities, an indication perhaps that the more conventional civic types are considered adequate. It should also be noted that almost half the "low" community ministers list no active participation in community associations.

TABLE 9

NON-CONGREGATIONAL ASSOCIATIONS: COMMUNITY, BY COMMUNITY TYPE

| Type of Association | Percentage of All Ministers | Percentage of Ministers by Type of Community | | |
|---|---|---|---|---|
| | | High | Middle | Low |
| Conventional civic | 35 | 41 | 29 | 45 |
| Area-wide, social action | 17 | 21 | 18 | 10 |
| Local community organization[a] | 44 | 66 | 45 | 10 |
| None at all[b] | 30 | 17 | 30 | 45 |
| No response | 6 | 3 | 7 | 5 |

[a] $x^2$ = 15.30; D.F. = 2; .001 level.

[b] $x^2$ = 4.78; D.F. = 2; .10 level.

Table 10 (Q, 25) presents the ranking of community activity relative to the other aspects of the ministry. The greatest concentration of ministers in any single ranking is the 80 percent of the "low" community ministers who say that community activity ranks fourth in time actually given--double the proportion of "middle" community ministers and over three times that of "high" community ministers. Roughly half the "high" community

TABLE 10

RANKING OF COMMUNITY ACTIVITY, BY COMMUNITY TYPE

| Rank | Percentage of All Ministers | Percentage of Ministers by Type of Community | | |
|---|---|---|---|---|
| | | High | Middle | Low |
| 1 | 13 | 17 | 14 | 5 |
| 2 | 12 | 21 | 13 | 0 |
| 3 | 19 | 24 | 20 | 10 |
| 4 | 43 | 24 | 39 | 80 |
| No response | 13 | 14 | 14 | 5 |
| Total | 100 | 100 | 100 | 100 |

$x^2$ = 15.22; D.F. = 4; .005 level ("1" and "2" rows combined).

ministers rank community activity either first or second, and half rank it either third or fourth; for the "middle" community ministers it is roughly one-third and two-thirds; and for the "low" community ministers it is roughly one-tenth and nine-tenths. This generalization can be checked by noting the ministers' estimate of the proportion of time they spend in community activity, as summarized in Table 11. (I, 11) On the basis of their own estimates, ministers in "high" communities spend considerably more of

TABLE 11

PERCENTAGE OF TIME IN COMMUNITY ACTIVITY, BY COMMUNITY TYPE

| Percentage of Time Spent | Percentage of All Ministers | Percentage of Ministers by Type of Community | | |
|---|---|---|---|---|
| | | High | Middle | Low |
| Less than 10 | 36 | 24 | 29 | 75 |
| 10-19 | 10 | 7 | 11 | 10 |
| 20-34 | 23 | 14 | 30 | 15 |
| More than 34 | 19 | 38 | 16 | 0 |
| No response | 12 | 17 | 14 | 0 |
| Total | 100 | 100 | 100 | 100 |

$x^2$ = 18.80; D.F. = 4; .001 level (excluding "10-19" row).

their time in community activity, than do ministers of the "low" communities In fact three-fourths of the latter group spend less than one-tenth of their time in community activity, while almost two-fifths of the former group spend more than one-third of their time in that type of activity. The "middle" group appears to be closer to the "high" than the "low" group in their participation.

The greatest "increase" in involvement is reported by the ministers of the "middle" communities (54 percent). Two-fifths of the ministers of the "low communities," despite their relatively low level of involvement in community activities, report that they are more involved than previously (on the other hand, almost half [45 percent] say that they are less involved than previously). A possible explanation is that, although ministers of "low" communities feel drawn into community affairs, the pressures of their congregational responsibilities confine them to the parochial type of participation. Less than one-tenth (9 percent) of the "middle" community ministers, and about one-fifth (21 percent) of those of the "high" communities report themselves as less involved. In giving the reasons for more or less involvement, the largest proportion of all ministers in all community types mention the "situation" or the "times."

Response to the statements designed to test the ministers' commitment to the given system of social organization and control shows general agreement across types of communities. The large majority of ministers tend to agree with those statements that challenge the status quo, and to disagree with those that support it. The exceptions, however, may be significant. For example, while only 1 percent of the ministers even "tend to" agree with the statement, "Things are pretty good nowadays, so it is best to keep things the way they are," 83 percent of the ministers of the "high" communities "strongly" disagree; just half of the ministers of the other two community types disagree to that extent.

Two other exceptions to the general agreement among community types are seen in Table 12. (Q, 19) There is ambiguity about the "American Way" in all community types, but there is considerably more disagreement with it in the "high" communities, and more agreement with it in the "low" communities. While the great majority of ministers in the "high" communities disagree that the experts should have priority over the people, the "low" community ministers are equally divided among those who agree and those who disagree. There is, however, no greater confidence in the decisions of the "people" generally in one community type or the other. Generally, the motivation for change would appear to be greatest among the "high" community ministers, although the openness to the possibility of change appears to be present among the ministers of all community types.

TABLE 12

SOCIETAL EVALUATION, BY COMMUNITY TYPE

| Statement | Evaluation | Percentage of All Ministers | Percentage of Ministers by Type of Community | | |
|---|---|---|---|---|---|
| | | | High | Middle | Low |
| America may not be perfect but the American Way has brought us about as close as human beings can get to a perfect society.[a] | Agree | 45 | 38 | 45 | 55 |
| | Disagree | 45 | 55 | 45 | 30 |
| | No response | 10 | 7 | 10 | 15 |
| | Total | 100 | 100 | 100 | 100 |
| In city planning the judgments of experts should have priority over the desires of people in local neighborhoods.[b] | Agree | 28 | 17 | 27 | 45 |
| | Disagree | 61 | 76 | 59 | 45 |
| | No response | 11 | 7 | 14 | 10 |
| | Total | 100 | 100 | 100 | 100 |

[a] $x^2 = 2.45$; D.F. = 2; $p > .10$.

[b] $x^2 = 5.26$; D.F. = 2; .10 level.

Table 13 (I, 2) indicates the problems which the ministers consider most urgent in their communities. The problem of "representation" is considered more urgent in "high" communities, that of "attitudes" in "low" communities. There is considerable urgency about "conditions" in both "high" and "middle" communities.

TABLE 13

MOST URGENT COMMUNITY PROBLEMS, BY COMMUNITY TYPE

| Problem Area | Percentage of All Ministers | Percentage of Ministers by Type of Community | | |
|---|---|---|---|---|
| | | High | Middle | Low |
| Responsibility for community | 21 | 14 | 23 | 25 |
| Representation of community | 15 | 38 | 9 | 0 |
| Attitudes toward community persons | 22 | 7 | 20 | 50 |
| Community conditions | 34 | 34 | 39 | 20 |
| Other problems | 5 | 3 | 5 | 5 |
| No response | 3 | 4 | 4 | 0 |
| Total | 100 | 100 | 100 | 100 |

$x^2 = 7.02$; D.F. = 6; $p > .10$ (excludes "other problems" row).

The ministers' analyses of the basic causes of the problems are summarized in Table 14.(I, 3) Most ministers in the "high" communities, no matter what they identify as the problem, attribute the cause at least in large measure to the prevailing "power allocation." Those who suffer the problems do not possess the power to alleviate the problems. Changes must be sought and made in that allocation of power. For the "middle" community ministers, the "new social situation" is seen as a basic cause. One may observe that among other things, the new social situation has caused the problems formerly experienced only by the "high" communities to be experienced now by the "middle" communities as well, and at least to threaten the "low" communities. Ministers in the "low" communities also cite "fears, prejudices" as basic causes, corresponding to their identification of "attitudes toward community persons" as an urgent community problem.

On the basis of their identification of different problems with different causes, we would expect the ministers of the various community types to have different evaluations of particular organizational responses to the problems. Ministers of the "low" communities favor in greatest proportion those organizations which tend to legitimate the given social and political organization, such as the YMCA, Billy Graham Crusade, and also those organizations which emphasize a sensitizing function, for instance the

TABLE 14

CAUSES OF COMMUNITY PROBLEMS, BY COMMUNITY TYPE

| Cause[a] | Percentage of All Ministers | Percentage of Ministers by Type of Community | | |
|---|---|---|---|---|
| | | High | Middle | Low |
| New social situation | 31 | 21 | 34 | 45 |
| Power allocation[b] | 34 | 76 | 21 | 0 |
| Public services | 9 | 10 | 13 | 0 |
| Qualifications of residents | 9 | 14 | 13 | 0 |
| Responsibility of residents | 19 | 14 | 21 | 10 |
| Fears, prejudices | 22 | 14 | 19 | 35 |
| Sin | 4 | 10 | 0 | 5 |
| No response | 3 | 3 | 4 | 10 |

[a]In some cases more than one cause was mentioned.

[b]$x^2$ = 41.6; D.F. = 2; .001 level.

Chicago Conference on Religion and Race. (One of the latter, The Metropolitan Chicago Leadership Council for Open Housing, was supported by about two-thirds of the ministers in all community types.) On the other hand those organizations which emphasize the politicizing function along with the sensitizing function, such as the Southern Christian Leadership Conference, and those which emphasize the politicizing function predominantly like The Woodlawn Organization, are favored in greatest proportion by ministers of the "high" communities.

It is also interesting to note that, while, as expected, the ministers of the "middle" communities generally are between the other two groups in their favoring or opposing, there is some variation here. For those organizations which are favored in greatest proportion by the "low" community ministers, the "middle" community ministers are closer to the "high" community ministers; for those organizations favored in greatest proportion by the "high" community ministers they are closer to the "low" community ministers. It can be suggested that while the "middle" community ministers have begun seriously to question more traditional approaches, they have not yet embraced the organizations which challenge the traditional approaches. Table 15 (Q, 18) illustrates the above summary, in the responses to two of the organizations.

TABLE 15

EVALUATION OF ORGANIZATIONS DEALING WITH PROBLEMS, BY COMMUNITY TYPE

| Organization, Evaluation | Percentage of All Ministers | Percentage of Ministers by Type of Community | | |
|---|---|---|---|---|
| | | High | Middle | Low |
| Lions, Kiwanis: favor | 31 | 31 | 27 | 45 |
| Chicago Urban League: favor | 57 | 72 | 50 | 55 |

What agencies do the ministers of the different community types consider to be most effective in dealing with urgent community problems? Table 16 (I, 5) provides data for this question. A small proportion of

TABLE 16

MOST EFFECTIVE AGENCY, BY COMMUNITY TYPE

| Type of Agency | Percentage of All Ministers | Percentage of Ministers by Type of Community | | |
|---|---|---|---|---|
| | | High | Middle | Low |
| A. Church Membership | | | | |
| Own congregation | 5 | 3 | 2 | 15 |
| Interdenominational associations | 13 | 10 | 16 | 10 |
| Denominational agencies | 0 | 0 | 0 | 0 |
| B. General Community Membership | | | | |
| Conventional civic organizations | 11 | 28 | 5 | 5 |
| Area-wide social action groups | 5 | 3 | 5 | 5 |
| Local community organizations | 34 | 38 | 41 | 10 |
| None at all, no response | 32 | 18 | 31 | 55 |
| Total | 100 | 100 | 100 | 100 |

$x^2 = 13.27$; D.F. = 2; .005 level ("local community organization," "none at all, no response" rows only).

ministers in all three types of communities identify church membership agencies as most effective. Somewhat over one-fourth of the ministers in the "high" areas consider conventional civic organizations as most effective, and over one-third consider local community organizations as most effective. About two-fifths of the "middle" community ministers consider local community organizations most effective.

It seems significant that over half the "low" community ministers feel that no agency is effectively dealing with community problems, and that it is in those communities that local community organizations are largely absent. The absence of effective agencies would account for much of the frustration felt by many of the "low" community ministers concerning their community participation. The relative lack of serious community problems, on the other hand, might account for their willingness to live with that frustration for the time being.

In analyzing the reason for the effectiveness of the agencies, Table 17, (I, 5a) the fairly even division of ministers between the two reasons, "organizational competence" (ability to achieve goals) and "communal adequacy," (adequate representation of community interests) carries across the community types. The exception is that the ministers of the "high" communities mention organizational competence, which we have identified more closely with the politicizing function, in somewhat greater proportion.

TABLE 17

REASONS FOR AGENCY EFFECTIVENESS, BY COMMUNITY TYPE

| Reason | Percentage of All Ministers | Percentage of Ministers by Type of Community: High | Middle | Low |
|---|---|---|---|---|
| Organizational competence | 35 | 48 | 34 | 20 |
| Communal adequacy | 33 | 34 | 36 | 25 |
| No response | 32 | 18 | 30 | 55 |
| Total | 100 | 100 | 100 | 100 |

$x^2$ = 10.11; D.F. = 2; .01 level.

What is the pattern of participation when we look beyond what the ministers are saying to what they are doing? Since there appears to be a difference in what the ministers in the different community types consider the most urgent problems, we would expect that the ministers would concentrate on different problems in their community activity. For example, the problems of "representation of community" and the underlying unequal "power allocation" were of much greater concern to the "high" community pastors, while "attitudes toward community persons" with their underlying "fears, prejudices" were of greater concern to the ministers of the "low" communities.

Their participation, according to Table 18 (I, 7) does seem to fulfill our expectations: "low" community ministers are mainly concerned in their activity with "attitudes," and also with "responsibility"; "high" community ministers are mainly concerned with "representation," and also with "conditions"; "middle" community ministers are mainly concerned with "conditions," and also with "responsibility."

TABLE 18

COMMUNITY PROBLEM AREA: PARTICIPATION, BY COMMUNITY TYPE

| Problem Area | Percentage of All Ministers | Percentage of Ministers by Type of Community: High | Middle | Low |
|---|---|---|---|---|
| Responsibility for community | 20 | 10 | 20 | 35 |
| Representation of community | 16 | 45 | 7 | 0 |
| Attitudes toward community persons | 16 | 7 | 13 | 40 |
| Community conditions | 32 | 24 | 41 | 20 |
| Other problems | 13 | 10 | 16 | 5 |
| No response | 3 | 4 | 3 | 0 |
| Total | 100 | 100 | 100 | 100 |

$x^2$ = 35.2; D.F. = 8; .001 level.

If the ministers participate through that agency which is most effective in dealing with the problem, in their judgment, we would expect high participation in local community organizations among the ministers of the "high" and "middle" communities. We recall that over half the ministers of the "low" communities could identify no agency as being effective. Table 19 (I, 7) shows in which agencies the ministers of the different types of community participate.

The local congregation is the agency of greatest participation for from one-third to one-half the ministers in all three community types, despite the fact that it is considered most effective by only 5 percent of all the ministers. The local community organization is the agency of greatest participation for exactly the same percentage of "high" community members as judge it most effective (38 percent). The percentage of "middle" community ministers who participate most actively in the local community organization, however, is somewhat lower than of those who consider it most effective (32 percent <u>vs</u>. 41 percent).

TABLE 19

AGENCY OF GREATEST INVESTMENT OF TIME,
BY COMMUNITY TYPE

| Type of Agency | Percentage of All Ministers | Percentage of Ministers by Type of Community | | |
|---|---|---|---|---|
| | | High | Middle | Low |
| A. Church Membership | | | | |
| Own congregation | 41 | 34 | 41 | 50 |
| Interdenominational associations | 19 | 10 | 14 | 45 |
| Denominational agencies | 0 | 0 | 0 | 0 |
| B. General Community Membership | | | | |
| Conventional civic organizations | 6 | 7 | 7 | 0 |
| Area-wide social action groups | 4 | 7 | 2 | 5 |
| Local community organizations | 28 | 38 | 32 | 0 |
| No response | 2 | 4 | 4 | 0 |
| Total | 100 | 100 | 100 | 100 |

$x^2$ = 9.57; D.F. = 4; .05 level ("own congregation," "interdenominational associations," "local community organizations" rows only).

Over half the ministers in the "high" communities participate most actively in general community membership agencies; about two-fifths of the "middle" community ministers, and one-twentieth of the "low" community ministers participate most actively in these groups. It should be stated, however, that interdenominational associations in the Chicago area do often bear the characteristics of the public style of participation; for instance, one of the suburban ("low") community ministerial associations had just sponsored a newspaper advertisement supporting open occupancy at the time of our interviews.

In stating their reasons for participating in the particular agency, Table 20, (I, 7) the majority of ministers in all three community types gave reasons having to do with adequacy to the community. However, almost two-fifths of the "high" community ministers mentioned reasons having to do with organizational competence, reflecting their greater sensitivity to the problem of power. The consideration of broader community is important to a greater proportion of "low" community ministers, reflecting their sensitivity to the problem of harmony among community members, including potential community members.

About half of the "high" and "middle" community ministers (48 percent and 55 percent) expressed a need for additional training for competence in dealing with social issues, but only about one-third (30 percent) of the "low" community ministers. Nevertheless, almost half (45 percent) of the latter group of ministers reported actually having taken special work to achieve such competence during the past five years, compared to a little over half (52 percent) for the "middle" community ministers and about three-fifths (62 percent) of the "high" community ministers.

TABLE 20

REASON FOR PARTICIPATION, BY COMMUNITY TYPE

| Reason[a] | Percentage of All Ministers | Percentage of Ministers by Type of Community | | |
|---|---|---|---|---|
| | | High | Middle | Low |
| Organizational competence[b] | 25 | 38 | 23 | 15 |
| Communal adequacy | 69 | 62 | 71 | 60 |
| Global community | 11 | 14 | 2 | 25 |
| No response | 4 | 4 | 4 | 0 |

[a]In some cases more than one reason was given.

[b]$x^2$ = 4.9; D.F. = 2; .10 level.

The summary index of "orientation to community problems" produces the results given in Table 21, when tabulated by community types.

Most of the "low" community ministers and two-fifths of the "middle" community ministers analyze and act in regard to community problems as if the main need is for the communities to organize themselves better for asserting the potential power for change that exists within the community ("assertive" orientation). About one-third of the "middle" community ministers, and almost two-thirds of the "high" community ministers think change in the social organization is necessary to give more power to the local communities ("transformative" orientation). There is a relatively low proportion of ministers in all community types with the "accommodative" orientation, which assumes that the main need is for individuals or communities to change themselves in order to qualify better for participation in society and its rewards.

TABLE 21

ORIENTATION TO COMMUNITY PROBLEMS, BY COMMUNITY TYPE

| Orientation | Percentage of All Ministers | Percentage of Ministers by Type of Community | | |
|---|---|---|---|---|
| | | High | Middle | Low |
| Accommodative | 18 | 14 | 21 | 10 |
| Assertive | 39 | 10 | 39 | 80 |
| Transformative | 36 | 62 | 30 | 10 |
| Combination of above | 3 | 10 | 4 | 0 |
| No response | 4 | 4 | 6 | 0 |
| Total | 100 | 100 | 100 | 100 |

$x^2 = 26.1$; D.F. = 4; .001 level (excludes "combinations" row).

## Summary

Our expectation concerning the public style, specified for the Chicago situation, was that the public style, while observable throughout the Chicago area, would be most observable in the lower class ghettoes, specifically on the south and west sides. These areas would correspond to our communities of "high" incidence of human welfare needs. The data presented in the preceding pages tend to validate this expectation, as well as the expectation that the public style would be least observable in the communities furthest from the city's center, and in its suburbs (the "low" communities). Thus, there does appear to be a difference of degree in the observation of the public style, according to the difference in community types.

We also stated the expectation that the public style would include cooperation not only with other ministers and parishes, but also with general community agents and groups; and, further, that it would be characterized more by activity either critical of or parallel to the given political organization, than by activity legitimating it. At the beginning of this chapter we found this to be generally the case. In this chapter we have seen that it is especially true of those ministers of the "high" communities, somewhat less so of those ministers in the "middle" communities, and considerably less so of those ministers in the "low" communities.

## The Denominational Factor

Is there any pattern in community participation that is related to the denominational membership of the ministers? It will be recalled that six denominations were represented in the survey: Episcopal; Lutheran Church in America; Lutheran Church-Missouri Synod; Methodist; United Church of Christ; United Presbyterian. All are distributed throughout the community units; all are Protestant; some have strong family ties within the history of Protestantism (e.g., the two Lutheran groups); but each is also a separately organized body, indicating the existence or perception of significant differences, which would raise the expectation of differences in ministry related to community.

When we examine the data in terms of denominations, however, the same continuum of responses observed for each variable is also observable within each denomination. That is, there is a variety of responses within each denomination, with the differences tending to be related to the type of community. The ministers of the Lutheran Church-Missouri Synod are the major exception. For most variables they tend, as a group, to be at the less active, more "parochial" end of the continuum, relative to community participation. The United Presbyterian ministers tend to be at the more active, more "public" end of the continuum, although they evidence a greater variety of responses as a group than do the Missouri Synod ministers.

The ministers of the other four denominations are found at various places in between, with no consistent pattern observable. The only thing that can be said is that the Lutheran Church in America and Methodist ministers are more often found closer to the United Presbyterian group, than are the ministers of the United Church of Christ and Episcopal denominations.[4] The following is only a selection of data to illustrate these observations.

In their preaching and teaching, Table 22 indicates that the Lutheran Church-Missouri Synod ministers, place great emphasis on the "inner life of faith and devotion," and relatively little emphasis on "members' responsibility in community life" and the "large social issues." The Lutheran Church in America group stands in marked contrast on each emphasis. The ministers of the Episcopal and United Church of Christ denominations tend toward the Missouri Synod ministers in their emphases (though less extremely so), while the ministers of the United Presbyterian and Methodist denominations tend toward the Lutheran Church in America ministers in their emphases.

On a specific social issue, ministers of all denominations are generally supportive of a "statewide open occupancy law." This is not the case in regard to "Negro housing protest demonstration marches in white neighborhoods," however, as observed in Table 23. In this table we can observe that in the Lutheran Church in America, Presbyterian, and Methodist groups, more ministers are supportive than non-supportive of the marches, but there is almost no support at all to be found among Lutheran Church-Missouri Synod ministers. Where the strategy is more within the given structure of change, e.g., open occupancy achieved by encouraging legislation, denominational variation is not apparent; where the strategy is outside of the given structure, especially if it carries the threat of disruption, variation does appear.

TABLE 22

PREACHING AND TEACHING EMPHASES, BY DENOMINATION (N=99)

| Subject, Emphasis | Percentage of All Ministers | Percentage of Ministers by Denomination[a] | | | | | |
|---|---|---|---|---|---|---|---|
| | | E | LCA | L-MS | M | UCC | UP |
| Inner life of faith and devotion[b] | | | | | | | |
| Much | 52 | 67 | 37 | 93 | 57 | 39 | 33 |
| Some | 33 | 33 | 47 | 7 | 38 | 33 | 27 |
| Little or no | 12 | 0 | 16 | 0 | 5 | 17 | 33 |
| No response | 3 | 0 | 0 | 0 | 0 | 11 | 7 |
| Total | 100 | 100 | 100 | 100 | 100 | 100 | 100 |
| Members' responsibility in community life[c] | | | | | | | |
| Much | 43 | 33 | 58 | 14 | 62 | 28 | 53 |
| Some | 51 | 67 | 42 | 65 | 38 | 61 | 40 |
| Little or no | 3 | 0 | 0 | 21 | 0 | 0 | 0 |
| No response | 3 | 0 | 0 | 0 | 0 | 11 | 7 |
| Total | 100 | 100 | 100 | 100 | 100 | 100 | 100 |
| Large social issues of the day[d] | | | | | | | |
| Much | 38 | 25 | 53 | 7 | 62 | 22 | 46 |
| Some | 49 | 67 | 47 | 43 | 38 | 61 | 40 |
| Little or no | 10 | 8 | 0 | 50 | 0 | 6 | 7 |
| No response | 3 | 0 | 0 | 0 | 0 | 11 | 7 |
| Total | 100 | 100 | 100 | 100 | 100 | 100 | 100 |

[a]In this and following tables denominations are designated as follows: E = Episcopal; LCA = Lutheran Church in America; L-MS = Lutheran Church, Missouri Synod; M = Methodist; UCC = United Church of Christ; UP = United Presbyterian.

[b]$x^2$ = 23.5; D.F. = 10; .02 level.

[c]$x^2$ = 27.2; D.F. = 10; .005 level.

[d]$x^2$ = 32.4; D.F. = 10; .001 level.

TABLE 23

ISSUE: NEGRO HOUSING MARCHES, BY DENOMINATION (N=99)

| Response | Percentage of All Ministers | Percentage of Ministers by Denomination | | | | | |
|---|---|---|---|---|---|---|---|
| | | E | LCA | L-MS | M | UCC | UP |
| Supportive | 36 | 33 | 42 | 7 | 52 | 33 | 40 |
| Non-supportive | 42 | 42 | 32 | 86 | 38 | 33 | 33 |
| Undecided, no response | 22 | 25 | 26 | 7 | 10 | 34 | 27 |
| Total | 100 | 100 | 100 | 100 | 100 | 100 | 100 |

Table 24 indicates the kind of community action in which ministers are involved. In the table, "congregational" action is again action taken within the congregation; "public: political" is action taken primarily within the official political system; "public: parapolitical" is action taken parallel to the official political system. The percentages indicate the ministers of each denomination who said they had participated in that kind of action during the past year.

TABLE 24

ACTION PARTICIPATED IN, BY DENOMINATION (N=99)

| Kind of Action | Percentage of All Ministers | Percentage of Ministers by Denomination | | | | | |
|---|---|---|---|---|---|---|---|
| | | E | LCA | L-MS | M | UCC | UP |
| Congregational | 92 | 100 | 95 | 86 | 100 | 78 | 100 |
| Public: political | 78 | 83 | 95 | 43 | 76 | 78 | 93 |
| Public: parapolitical[a] | 60 | 58 | 79 | 14 | 71 | 61 | 67 |
| All three kinds[b] | 55 | 58 | 74 | 7 | 62 | 56 | 67 |
| None at all | 6 | 0 | 0 | 14 | 0 | 17 | 0 |
| No response | 0 | 0 | 0 | 0 | 0 | 0 | 0 |

[a] $x^2$ = 13.05; D.F. = 5; .025 level.

[b] $x^2$ = 13.14; D.F. = 5; .10 level.

In that category of action which most bears the appearance of the public style, "public: parapolitical," the proportions of ministers in the Lutheran Church in America, Methodist, and United Presbyterian denominations are again larger than those of the other three. The United Church of Christ and Episcopal percentages are not much lower, however. The percentage of the Lutheran Church-Missouri Synod ministers is markedly lower.

The differences that exist among denominations are also observable. The rankings of community activity relative to the position it "ought to have," and the position it "actually has" are reproduced in Table 25.

If one combines the percentages for first and second in both categories there is a general consistency between the rank the ministers think community activity "ought to have" and what it "actually" does have. In other words about the same percentage of ministers in all denominations (except the United Church of Christ) who think community activity "ought to have" first or second place "actually" give it first or second place. The greatest contrast observable in the rankings is between the ministers of the United Presbyterian congregations and those of the Missouri Synod. Almost one-half of the former say that community activity both "ought to have" and "actually" does have first or second ranking in their ministries. None at all of the latter give community activity these rankings in either category.

TABLE 25

RANKING OF COMMUNITY ACTIVITY, BY DENOMINATION (N=99)

| Ranking | | Percentage of All Ministers | Percentage of Ministers by Denomination | | | | | |
|---|---|---|---|---|---|---|---|---|
| | | | E | LCA | L-MS | M | UCC | UP |
| Ought to have | 1 | 10 | 0 | 11 | 0 | 10 | 17 | 20 |
| | 2 | 21 | 33 | 26 | 0 | 24 | 17 | 27 |
| | 3 | 34 | 0 | 37 | 21 | 43 | 22 | 20 |
| | 4 | 28 | 67 | 21 | 79 | 14 | 33 | 27 |
| No response | | 7 | 0 | 5 | 0 | 9 | 11 | 6 |
| Total | | 100 | 100 | 100 | 100 | 100 | 100 | 100 |
| Actually has[a] | 1 | 14 | 8 | 16 | 0 | 14 | 11 | 33 |
| | 2 | 14 | 25 | 26 | 0 | 14 | 6 | 13 |
| | 3 | 19 | 50 | 10 | 14 | 10 | 28 | 13 |
| | 4 | 45 | 17 | 42 | 86 | 48 | 44 | 33 |
| No response | | 8 | 0 | 5 | 0 | 14 | 11 | 8 |
| Total | | 100 | 100 | 100 | 100 | 100 | 100 | 100 |

[a] $x^2$ = 21.9; D.F. = 10; .02 level ("1" and "2" rankings only).

When we look at "percentage of time" spent in community activity, Table 26, the contrast between United Presbyterian and Lutheran Church-Missouri Synod ministers is again very marked. The similarity between Methodist and United Presbyterian ministers is also apparent; but the Lutheran Church in America ministers resemble those of the United Church of Christ and Episcopal denominations more closely, especially in the "35 percent and over" category.

TABLE 26

PERCENTAGE OF TIME IN COMMUNITY ACTIVITY, BY DENOMINATION (N=102)

| Percentage of Time Spent | Percentage of All Ministers | Percentage of Ministers by Denomination | | | | | |
|---|---|---|---|---|---|---|---|
| | | E | LCA | L-MS | M | UCC | UP |
| Less than 20 | 45 | 46 | 45 | 88 | 27 | 37 | 33 |
| 20-34 | 23 | 24 | 35 | 6 | 32 | 19 | 20 |
| 35 and over | 20 | 15 | 15 | 0 | 32 | 19 | 40 |
| No response | 12 | 15 | 5 | 6 | 9 | 25 | 7 |
| Total | 100 | 100 | 100 | 100 | 100 | 100 | 100 |

In terms of the "most urgent community problem," we have previously grouped the problems into four areas: responsibility for community; representation of community; attitudes toward community persons; and community conditions. There are ministers in each of the denominations who cite each of the problems, except that none of the Missouri Synod ministers cite "representation of community." The larger number of those ministers cite "community attitudes" and "community conditions." This is also the case with the Lutheran Church in America ministers. The larger number of United Presbyterian ministers cite "attitudes" and "representation," and of the Methodist and Episcopal ministers "conditions" and "responsibility." Half the United Church of Christ ministers cite "conditions."

In articulating basic causes of community problems, the Presbyterian and Lutheran Church in America ministers seem to be most sensitive to the "allocation of power"; Missouri Synod ministers seem least sensitive to this cause. The largest proportion of Episcopal, Methodist, and United Church of Christ ministers see the cause as resting in the "new social situation" for which old ways of response are not adequate. Both of these causes reflect an inadequacy in the sensitizing function, while the "allocation of power" is the cause which most directly involves the politicizing function.

Three-fourths of the Lutheran Church-Missouri Synod ministers are personally most involved with the problems of responsibility and attitudes, both of which can be addressed within the congregational structure. On the other hand, none of them focus their involvement on the problem of representation, which is probably the one which can least be dealt with in the parochial style, while one-third of the Presbyterian ministers do.

In their evaluations of the effectiveness of various kinds of organizations dealing with community problems, few ministers of any of the denominations rate local congregations, denominational agencies or area-wide social action groups as the most effective agency. Episcopalian ministers name interdenominational agencies as most effective in greater proportion than any of the others; Methodist ministers name conventional civic organizations in greatest proportion. Lutheran Church in America, Episcopal, and United Presbyterian ministers are most supportive of local community organizations. Half the Missouri Synod ministers are unable to name any organization as most effective; but most who are able to, name local community organizations.

In Table 27 we observe the agencies in which the ministers of the various denominations invest the greatest amount of their time. Those agencies in Group B are most likely to fulfill the politicizing and sensitizing functions. Only one-fourth of the Missouri Synod ministers have

TABLE 27

AGENCY OF GREATEST INVESTMENT OF TIME, BY DENOMINATION (N=102)

| Type of Agency | Percentage of All Ministers | Percentage of Ministers by Denomination | | | | | |
|---|---|---|---|---|---|---|---|
| | | E | LCA | L-MS | M | UCC | UP |
| Group A | | | | | | | |
| Own congregation | 40 | 23 | 25 | 69 | 38 | 50 | 33 |
| Denominational agencies | 0 | 0 | 0 | 0 | 0 | 0 | 0 |
| Conventional civic organizations | 7 | 0 | 10 | 6 | 5 | 6 | 13 |
| Group B | | | | | | | |
| Interdenominational associations | 20 | 54 | 25 | 6 | 28 | 6 | 7 |
| Area-wide social action groups | 4 | 8 | 0 | 0 | 5 | 6 | 7 |
| Local community organizations | 29 | 15 | 40 | 19 | 24 | 32 | 40 |
| No response | 0 | 0 | 0 | 0 | 0 | 0 | 0 |
| Total | 100 | 100 | 100 | 100 | 100 | 100 | 100 |

their greatest participation in this category, while for 69 percent, the congregation is the agency of greatest participation. Of the other five denominations, only the United Church of Christ has a majority of ministers for whom the greatest investment of time is Group A. One notes that interdenominational agencies receive the greatest share of time for over half the Episcopal ministers, and community organizations receive the greatest share of time for two-fifths of the Lutheran Church in America and Presbyterian ministers. The congregation is the agency receiving the greatest investment of time in community participation for at least 20 percent of the ministers in all denominations.

The final aspect of our analysis of the style of participation in the community was general "orientation to community problem areas." The "accommodative" orientation carries greatest legitimation of the organizational status quo of society. The "transformative" orientation carries the least. The "assertive" orientation does legitimate the system as a whole, but not the way it is working at present. Both the assertive and transformative orientations include a strong awareness of the need for giving attention to the sensitizing and politicizing functions of the society. Table 28 summarizes this factor by denomination.

TABLE 28

ORIENTATION TO COMMUNITY PROBLEMS, BY DENOMINATION (N=102)

| Orientation[a] | Percentage of All Ministers | Percentage of Ministers by Denomination: E | LCA | L-MS | M | UCC | UP |
|---|---|---|---|---|---|---|---|
| Accommodative | 18 | 0 | 11 | 38 | 23 | 37 | 13 |
| Assertive | 40 | 77 | 47 | 50 | 27 | 25 | 27 |
| Tranformative | 37 | 15 | 42 | 12 | 50 | 19 | 53 |
| Combination of above | 5 | 8 | 0 | 0 | 0 | 19 | 7 |
| Total | 100 | 100 | 100 | 100 | 100 | 100 | 100 |

[a] $x^2$ = 24.2; D.F. = 10; .01 level (excluding "combination" row).

The greatest concentration in any one orientation is the three-fourths of the Episcopal ministers in the assertive orientation. Some ministers in each denomination are found in each orientation, with the exception that there are no Episcopal ministers in the accommodative orientation. There is a different alignment of denominations in the three highest and three lowest in each orientation; in the "transformative," however, the highest percentages are in the Lutheran Church in America, Methodist, and Presbyterian columns (42-53 percent). The range for the other three denominations is considerably lower (12-19 percent).

Comparing the data on the denominational factor with those on the community factor, the latter would seem to be the stronger in conditioning the degree and content of the public style. To the extent that our data can be generalized, we might expect that ministers as a group would manifest the public style most strongly in the communities of high welfare need. Within the communities we might expect that Presbyterian ministers would take the lead in pursuing this style, while ministers of the Lutheran Church-Missouri Synod would give only token support. Ministers of the Methodist churches and those of the Lutheran Church in America would perhaps be most ready to follow the lead of the Presbyterian ministers, with somewhat greater hesitancy to be found among the Episcopal and United Church of Christ ministers. Exceptions to these generalizations would be expected, particularly with respect to denomination. Nevertheless, these general tendencies are observable in our sample.

## The Public and Parochial Styles

To this point we have presented data indicating the presence of the "public style" of community participation throughout most of our sample. The degree to which it is present varies greatly. The type of community in which the minister works seems to have much to do with the degree to which the public style is present. Denominational membership also appears to be a factor, but not as strong as that of the community.

As a way of focusing more sharply the concept of the public style, and by contrast the parochial style, we will identify a group of ministers who appear most consistently to express the two styles of participation. If we take the congregation and the community as the two foci of ministry, and the parochial and the public as the two styles of ministry, the following initial breakdown of the survey of ministers can be made. The style of the majority of the ministers is of a parochial/public type: parochial in relation to the congregation, public in relation to the community (to varying extents). There are some, however, who are of a parochial/parochial type of style, that is, parochial in relation to both congregation and community. And there are some who are of a public/public type of style, that is, public in relation to both congregation and community.

The latter two groups provide "ideal types" of the most consistent expression of the two styles. To give some precision to our identification, we have included in the public/public group only those ministers who: (1) rank "community activity" either 1st or 2nd in terms both of the priority it ought to have and actually does have relative to the other more parochial aspects of the ministry; (2) who spend 35 percent or more of their time in community activity; and (3) who have participated in what we have referred to as "action taken parallel to the official political system" (cf. Table 12, Group C). The parochial/parochial group includes only those ministers who (1) rank community activity 4th, behind the more parochial aspects of the ministry, both in terms of the priority it ought to have and actually does have; (2) who spend less than 20 percent of their time in community activity; and (3) who have not participated in parapolitical action.

These criteria identify fourteen representatives of the public style and fifteen representatives of the parochial style, each group thus constituting about 15 percent of the total sample of respondents. Distribution by denomination and community type is given in Table 29.

The public style is generally distributed across the denominations in close proportion to the denomination's presence in the sample. Exceptions to be noted are that the Lutheran Church-Missouri Synod is totally unrepresented, and the Methodist and United Presbyterian denominations are represented in somewhat greater proportion than their representation in the total sample. In the parochial style the Missouri Synod is represented in far greater proportion than its presence in the total sample; the United Church is represented in about the same proportion; while the other denominations are represented in lesser proportion. This tends to support our previous conclusions about denomination and style of community participation, especially regarding the Lutheran Church-Missouri Synod.

TABLE 29

PUBLIC-PAROCHIAL STYLE: DISTRIBUTION

| | Percentage of Ministers[a] | | |
|---|---|---|---|
| | Total Sample | Public Style | Parochial Style |
| Denomination | | | |
| Episcopal | 12.4 | 7.1 | 0.0 |
| Lutheran-LCA | 19.0 | 21.4 | 6.7 |
| Lutheran-L-MS | 16.2 | 0.0 | 60.0 |
| Methodist | 21.0 | 28.6 | 6.7 |
| United Presbyterian | 14.3 | 21.4 | 6.7 |
| United Church of Christ | 17.1 | 21.4 | 20.0 |
| Total | 100.0 | 99.9 | 100.1 |
| Community Type[b] | | | |
| High | 27.6 | 71.4 | 26.7 |
| Middle | 53.4 | 28.6 | 40.0 |
| Low | 19.0 | 0.0 | 33.3 |
| Total | 100.0 | 100.0 | 100.0 |

[a] In the tables in this section, N = 14 for "public style" and N = 15 for "parochial style." Because of the smaller numbers involved, percentages are carried to the nearest tenth, with totals therefore varying from 99.9 to 100.1.

[b] KS test: $D = 6.3$; $p > .05$.

The <u>public</u> style is associated with the "high" community type in far greater proportion than that community type is present in the total sample. The distribution of the <u>parochial</u> style, on the other hand, is distributed much more in proportion across the community types. One would conclude from these tables that the public style, in its most consistent manifestation, is most closely associated with community type, with some association with denomination. The parochial style, in its most consistent manifestation, is most closely associated with denomination, with some association with community type.

Among the memberships of the congregations of the two groups of ministers, little difference exists in the amount of their education, type of occupation and proximity of residence to the church. There are differences to be noted in size, age, and racial makeup of memberships, as observable in Table 30.

There appears to be a tendency for the congregations of ministers representing the public style to be smaller, and for their members to be younger and black. The age and racial makeup reflect the high proportion of these congregations in the "high" community types which are predominantly black and younger. Also, the congregations of the predominantly white Protestant denominations tend to be smaller in these areas. But in addition the smaller membership would suggest that the minister of such a congregation would have more time for the public style, while larger memberships almost demand the parochial style.

The pattern of membership trends in congregations is also included in Table 30. One would expect that congregations in the "high" community types would be decreasing in membership, that perhaps the public style would be at the cost of building up institutional membership. The large percentage of congregations showing a trend toward decreasing membership in the "public style" column, therefore, is not surprising. But it is surprising that half the congregations in that column show a trend toward increasing membership, compared with only one-third in the "parochial style" columns.

When we look at the ministers themselves, Table 31, those representing the public style tend to be younger and their tenure in their present congregations tends to be shorter than those representing the parochial style. In addition, approximately one-fourth of the public style ministers are black; all of the other group are white. There is almost no difference in the size of the community in which the minister spent his pre-college years; about four-fifths of both groups grew up in non-metropolitan communities (less than 100,000 population).

The public style would seem to be associated most with an assertive or transformative orientation to community change. The accommodative orientation, stressing the need for upgrading individual motivation and qualification would be quite compatible with the parochial style. Table 32 presents the distribution of these orientations.

TABLE 30

PUBLIC-PAROCHIAL STYLE: CONGREGATIONS

| | Percentage of Ministers | |
|---|---|---|
| | Public Style | Parochial Style |
| Membership of Congregations[a] | | |
| Less than 150 members | 35.7 | 0.0 |
| 150 to 499 members | 57.1 | 60.0 |
| Over 500 members | 7.1 | 40.0 |
| Total | 99.9 | 100.0 |
| Racial Makeup of Membership[b] | | |
| All or mostly Negro | 64.3 | 6.7 |
| About half Negro and half Caucasian | 7.1 | 0.0 |
| Mostly Caucasian | 7.1 | 13.3 |
| All Caucasian | 21.4 | 80.0 |
| Total | 99.9 | 100.0 |
| Age of Membership[c] | | |
| Less than 50 percent over 50 years | 85.7 | 46.7 |
| 50 percent and more over 50 years | 14.3 | 53.3 |
| Total | 100.0 | 100.0 |
| Trend of Membership[d] | | |
| Membership decreasing | 42.9 | 26.7 |
| Membership remaining the same | 7.1 | 40.0 |
| Membership increasing | 50.0 | 33.3 |
| Total | 100.0 | 100.0 |

[a]KS test: D = 5.04; $p > .05$.

[b]KS test: D = 9.1; .01 level.

[c]$x_y^2 = 5.1$; D.F. = 1; .025 level.

[d]KS test: D = 2.4; $p > .05$.

TABLE 31

PUBLIC-PAROCHIAL STYLE: MINISTERS

| | Percentage of Ministers | |
|---|---|---|
| | Public Style | Parochial Style |
| Age of Ministers[a] | | |
| Under 35 years | 64.3 | 20.0 |
| 35 to 44 years | 21.4 | 26.7 |
| 45 to 54 years | 7.1 | 20.0 |
| Over 54 years | 7.1 | 33.4 |
| Total | 99.9 | 100.1 |
| Tenure of Ministers[b] | | |
| Five years or less | 85.7 | 46.7 |
| Five to ten years | 7.1 | 26.7 |
| Over ten years | 7.1 | 26.7 |
| Total | 99.9 | 100.0 |

[a]KS test: D = 6; $p > .05$.

[b]KS test: D = 5.5; $p > .05$.

TABLE 32

PUBLIC-PAROCHIAL STYLE: ORIENTATION TO SOCIAL CHANGE

| | Percentage of Ministers | |
|---|---|---|
| Orientation[a] | Public Style | Parochial Style |
| Accommodative | 0.0 | 53.3 |
| Assertive | 0.0 | 40.0 |
| Transformative | 100.0 | 6.7 |
| Total | 100.0 | 100.0 |

[a]KS test: D = 13; .01 level.

Actually the orientation of all of the representatives of the public style is transformative, and only half of those of the parochial style is accommodative. This would suggest a factor which moves the former toward the transformative, beyond the assertive, and a factor which restrains some of the latter from more active participation despite an orientation which really encourages it. We have already noted the strength of the denominational factor in the parochial style and of the situational factor in the public style. At this point we will indicate something of the theological content which we would assume underlies and perhaps reinforces the strength of the denominational and situational factors.

In the interviews, the ministers were asked, "When you are asked by members of the congregation to explain the connection between [the particular community problem and/or activity in which engaged] and the work of the church, how do you answer?" (I, 8). If not included in their initial response we asked about "specific theological doctrines or Biblical teachings," and specifically about the "concept of 'God's saving work.'" In analyzing the responses of the two groups of ministers we are presently considering, we found that almost all of the ministers were prepared to justify the high or low priority they gave to community activity, within their understanding of the "work of the church." Exceptions were one representative of the "public style" who considered his community participation as just something that needed doing--as compatible with, but not essential to, the work of the church as such, and two representatives of the "parochial style" who felt that they should be spending more time in community participation, even though not ready to give it higher ranking.

We also found that the representatives of the parochial style did indeed see the connection between the work of the church and the quality of social life to be indirect. The concern of the church is the quality of the life of the individual, who in turn contributes to the quality of social life through his individual role in society. Further, in explaining the relatively low degree of participation within that understanding, two-thirds of this group cited the institutional demands upon their time. This implies, and a number of these ministers said it explicitly, that the concern for the quality of the life of individuals is largely expressed through the institutional program of preaching and teaching.

The representatives of the public style, on the other hand, see a direct connection between the work of the church and the quality of social life. This concern must be intentionally a part of, and if necessary must precede, the concern for the quality of individual life. Three-fourths of this group of ministers, in explaining the degree of participation within this understanding, cited demands related to the specific situation and the general times in which they ministered. This implies, and a number of these ministers said it explicitly, that the concern for the quality of social life is expressed in large measure, though not exclusively, outside the institutional program.

The ministers' identification of their theological positions in terms of "popular labels" listed in the questionnaire (Q, 36) puts most of the parochial style ministers at the more traditional or conservative end of the spectrum, and most of the public style ministers at the more contemporary or liberal end of the spectrum. In Table 33, public style ministers who checked "other" in the questionnaire specified the "other" with such labels as "renewal" and "ecumenical." The table, combined with the analysis of the ministers' articulation of the grounding of their participation, gives some support to a continued identification of an institutionally-oriented ministry with a conservative or traditional theology, and of a socially-oriented ministry with a liberal or contemporary theology.

TABLE 33

PUBLIC-PAROCHIAL STYLE: THEOLOGICAL POSITION

| | Percentage of Ministers | |
|---|---|---|
| Position[a] | Public Style | Parochial Style |
| Fundamentalist | 0.0 | 6.7 |
| Conservative | 14.3 | 46.7 |
| Neo-orthodox | 0.0 | 26.7 |
| Liberal | 35.7 | 13.3 |
| Other | 50.0 | 6.7 |
| Total | 100.0 | 100.1 |

[a]KS test: D = 9.2; .01 level ("liberal" and "other" rows combined).

Since the public style is a departure from the more expected style of participation for American ministers, it might well raise problems about the minister's relation to members of his congregation, his denomination, and his community. We asked the ministers, "In your ministry, do you feel that you are moving along the same lines as your denomination?" (I, 17). Some felt, see Table 34, they were moving along the same lines, others felt they lagged "behind" the denomination in community participation, with the stipulation either that the denomination was nevertheless correct or that the denomination was moving too far in that direction, while still others felt that they were ahead of the denomination.

From the proportion of parochial style representatives who feel they are behind their denominations and that of the public style representatives who feel they are with the denomination, it would appear that denominations themselves are moving toward the public style. Nevertheless over half of the public style representatives see themselves as ahead of the denominations. (A source of current power struggles within denominations is evident here.) The representatives of the public style are conscious of more denominational encouragement, mostly in terms of the denominations' sanction of what they are doing and financial support; but neither those who are ahead of or behind their denominations are conscious of denominational pressures to conform to a particular denominational "line."

TABLE 34

PUBLIC-PAROCHIAL STYLE: RELATION TO DENOMINATIONAL STANCE

| | Percentage of Ministers | |
|---|---|---|
| Relation[a] | Public Style | Parochial Style |
| Same as denomination | 35.7 | 40.0 |
| Behind denomination, but denomination right | 0.0 | 33.3 |
| Behind denomination, but denomination wrong | 0.0 | 20.0 |
| Ahead of denomination | 57.1 | 6.7 |
| No response | 7.1 | 0.0 |
| Total | 99.9 | 100.0 |

[a]KS test: D = 7.4; .03 level.

The ministers also responded to the question, "Have the members of the congregation expressed themselves concerning your community activity--the amount of time you spend this way, the stands you've taken, or your being involved at all?" (I, 12). It is interesting to note that only one-fifth of the representatives of the parochial style felt they had the active approval of their congregations, while half the other group did. On the other hand, none of the former felt any opposition to their style of participation, while a third of the latter did. The public style can thus win the support of congregations, as well as stir up opposition. And while there is indeed a clergy-lay split within denominations, it probably needs to be more carefully defined to reveal the split that runs across the clergy and lay groups, with some of both to be found on each side.

About a third of the representatives of the public style felt that they received more support from the local community than from their congregations. Most of the representatives of both styles, however, felt that the general community gave the same degree of support as their congregations. More than half of the public style representatives had received pressures of various kinds from economic or political interests of the community because of their community participation. Only one of the other group had, not surprisingly the one with the transformative orientation to community change.

Another important factor regarding support of the public style is the support received from fellow ministers. The fourteen public style ministers are located in seven different community areas, and only four of them are the only public style representatives in their communities. Five of them are in one community area, Woodlawn, and include all but one of that area's ministers in our sample. Three of the men are from the Garfield Park area, and two from the Lincoln Park area. There is at least communication among the representatives in the same communities, and in most cases a strong week-to-week working relationship.

On the other hand the fifteen parochial style ministers are located in eleven different community areas, eight of them being the only parochial style representatives in their communities. There are two representatives in each of two community areas, and three in one area. However, there is no indication of anything more than acquaintance among these latter ministers, except in one case where two of the men are from the same denomination. Even here, however, it is not a local working relationship. The parochial style of participation is one which almost by definition can be carried on independently of other ministers. The public style, on the other hand, almost demands the encouragement and structures which can be provided by colleagues.

How comfortable and competent do the ministers feel in their style of ministry? Most of the ministers of both styles (about three-fourths of the public, and nine-tenths of the parochial) said that they would choose to be in their present type of ministry if they were to have their choice, e.g., inner city parish, suburban parish, etc. (Q, 27). In addition most of both styles had a generally positive evaluation of their participation in the problems and issues of the community. In fact all of the representatives of the public style did, while there were about one-third of the other group who had a negative evaluation; they did not feel that what they were doing was effective, even though right for them. There is a somewhat greater correlation between the public style and sense of efficacy in relation to community participation, although not of satisfaction with type of ministry.

Over two-thirds of the ministers representing the public style felt "the need for . . . types of training in the seminary program that were not available when you were a student" (Q, 34). Of those who did not feel the need, all graduated from seminary before 1960, of those who did, all but two graduated from seminary after 1960. The more recent graduates do not feel that the seminary is preparing them adequately for this style of ministry. Of these most expressed the desire for training in the social sciences, community relations, and related fields.

About three-fifths of the representatives of the parochial style also expressed the need for additional training, but mainly in the fields of psychology, interpersonal relations, and related fields. Only a third had taken additional training in the social sciences, etc., while four-fifths of the ministers representing the public style had.

Do representatives of the public style feel a continuing "inclination toward the more parochial style?" None of those few who said they would choose a different type of ministry if the choice were given them indicated a type where a more parochial style might be possible. In addition two-thirds of them said that events or accomplishments related to community activity had been most significant in their total ministry during the past year. Perhaps this only corroborates what one might expect, that one would not voluntarily commit himself so fully to a style of ministry with which he was not comfortable, or from which he did not derive great satisfaction. It should be recalled that these men were convinced that community activity should have a high priority, and in addition many of them stated that they felt they were best meeting the parochial interests of the congregation through the public style.

## Summary

Consideration of this sub-sample of the ministers indicates again that the public style tends to be associated with the "high" welfare need type of community, while the parochial style tends to be associated with the Lutheran Church-Missouri Synod. There is no strong single denominational tendency for the public style nor single community type tendency for the parochial style.

A number of additional factors are suggested as at least worth noting in describing the styles. For example, the public style is associated with congregations which tend to be smaller and younger in membership and with a higher proportion of black members than those of ministers using the parochial style. The parochial style is associated with ministers who tend to be older and have a longer tenure in their present parish than those of the public style. Orientation to social change is exclusively transformative for the public style ministers, while the parochial style ministers are found almost exclusively in the assertive and accommodative orientations.

Ministers of the public style see a direct connection between their theological understanding of the work of the church and the quality of social life, while for the parochial style group it is an indirect connection. The former group place themselves at the more liberal or contemporary end of the theological spectrum; the latter place themselves at the more conservative or traditional end. Ministers of the parochial style tend to work more independently of other ministers than do those of the public style. Ministers of both styles appear to be satisfied with their own style, for their own ministry.

In the following chapter we shall look at the community participation of specific ministers, among whom are included representatives of the two groups whom we have been discussing.

# CHAPTER IV

## PROFILES OF PARTICIPATION

In this chapter we attempt to describe in non-statistical ways the individuality of ministries and the characteristics of particular situations, associations and activities. We will describe three communities, one for each type, and the community participation of three ministers of each. The description of the communities is based on published material, supplemented by information received from the ministers, and the observations of the writer. The primary source for the descriptions of the ministers' participation is the survey interviews, supplemented by the questionnaires.

The specific communities have been chosen to include as much as possible of the range of community problems, associations, denominations, and styles of participation represented in the preceding chapter. The actual names of community units, organizations, and programs are used. In order to preserve the anonymity promised the ministers, however, the men will not be identified by their own names, the names of their congregations or their denominations. They will be identified simply as Rev. A, B, . . . consecutively.

### East-West Garfield Park

The community areas of East and West Garfield Park begin at about 2600 West and extending to about 4600 West. The Eisenhower Expressway, linking the Loop with the western suburbs and the Tri-State Tollway, runs through the lower half of the communities. Garfield Park, one of the major city parks, runs north and south down the center, although it is included in the East Garfield Park community boundaries.

The Garfield Park communities have a "high" incidence of human welfare needs. The summer of our study, a Chicago Sun-Times article, "The City's Sensitive Spots," gave the following terse description of them:

> East Garfield Park--Taylor to Chicago and North Western Ry., Rockwell to Hamlin--part of the 1966 riot area. 20 percent under $3,000, 30 percent on welfare.
>
> West Garfield Park--Taylor to Chicago and North Western Ry., Hamlin to Kolmar--scene of violence in 1965 after a fire truck killed a woman. 15 percent under $3,000, 30 percent on welfare. 12 percent on public assistance.[1]

In a way these brief descriptions say it all--massive human need, plus violent response to the conditions of need. What the descriptions do not say, however, is that the present state of these communities is a largely post-war phenomenon. Before World War II they were predominantly white residential communities. After the War they became a part of the black ghetto expansion which had previously been confined to the south side of Chicago. East Garfield Park changed first, and by 1966 was estimated to be 87.5 percent non-white in population (54,820 persons), compared with the 4.6 percent (3,085 persons) reported in the 1940 census.

It was thought that Garfield Park itself would serve as a barrier to further westward expansion of the ghetto, but by 1966 West Garfield Park was estimated to be 68.7 percent non-white. The rapidity of change is demonstrated by the following statistics for that area:

1950: percentage non-white 0.2 (115 persons)
1960: percentage non-white 16.4 (7,459 persons)
1966: percentage non-white 68.7 (29,107 persons)

As the percentage of non-white population has increased, the indices of human welfare needs have climbed, and the preparation and organization to deal with those needs have declined.

Total population has been decreasing in the two areas over the past fifteen years. Total population in East Garfield Park was 70,091 in 1950, 66,871 in 1960, with an estimated population of 62,652 in 1966. The corresponding figures for West Garfield Park are 48,443, 45,611, and 42,368. East Garfield Park is among the fifteen community areas highest in all human welfare needs indices. West Garfield Park ranks somewhat lower, but is still at the high end of the incidence scale.

We interviewed five ministers in the communities. Of the community problems listed in the questionnaire, there was no more than one that was not considered to be serious by each minister. Two of the ministers checked every one as serious. All of them considered "ineffective political representation" to be a serious problem. Political representation has not changed with the change in racial composition. In the 1967 aldermanic election a white, machine-backed candidate defeated a black independent candidate, in the predominantly black area.

The community organizations of long standing also seem to represent the older political and business interests rather than the new residential interests. There is among the residents, therefore, according to the ministers, neither the power nor the sense of community. Alternative community organizing efforts have been undertaken in both areas to build community and power, as means to changing conditions.

The minority position of the predominantly white Protestant denominations in these communities is obvious in the listing of community churches. In East Garfield Park there are about forty Baptist congregations, none of which is affiliated with the American or Southern Baptist Conventions, plus numerous Churches of God in Christ, three Roman Catholic churches, one Methodist, one United Church of Christ, and one Presbyterian congregation.

In West Garfield Park, it is about the same, with the addition of several American and Southern Baptist Convention churches, one Lutheran Church in America and one Episcopal congregation.

In West Garfield Park the Christian Action Mission (CAM) is a cooperative action program of seven congregations, including two Roman Catholic and one black Baptist. CAM came into being in 1965, as a response of some ministers to the riot that summer. A minister acts as the convenor of CAM. There is a paid full-time director. In addition there are a number of OEO-financed workers attached to CAM. Much of the financial support comes from denominational funds of the participating congregations. Included in the CAM structure are committees on housing, employment (there is an OEO-financed employment center located in one of the churches), tutoring, cultural enrichment, counseling, and recreation. The CAM Academy is a school for high school dropouts, and receives material assistance from the Encyclopedia Britannica Company.

Another part of the church situation is the Ecumenical Institute, the headquarters of which are in East Garfield Park. A part of the Institute program is the "Fifth City" project, focused on the surrounding community. The ministers in our sample, however, were not involved in this project.

All of the congregations whose ministers we interviewed have been in the Garfield Park area for more than fifty years. All of them have memberships of fewer than 300, three of them fewer than 150. Two ministers report increasing memberships, two decreasing memberships, and one a membership remaining about the same during the past five years. In both cases of increasing membership the congregations had decreased significantly in membership and are now being built up in relation to a new pastor's style of ministry. At least 75 percent of the members of these two congregations live within a mile of the church building.

Four of the congregations' memberships have fewer than 25 percent over fifty years in age. All of them have memberships with fewer than 25 percent having two years or more college education, and three of them have 75 percent or more of their members in blue collar occupations. The racial makeup of four of the five churches is mostly black. One of the church buildings was undergoing a major renovation. Four of the five churches receive denominational financial aid.

One of the five ministers was going to retire later that same year, and had been in his parish more than ten years. The other four had been in their present congregations five years or less. Three of them were under thirty-five years of age.

With this general background of the Garfield Park community and church situation, we shall consider individually the community participation of three of its ministers.

Rev. A. listed the whole gamut of community problems, ending with the fact that the "people in this community don't control their community. They don't participate in the decision-making process." He considers the most urgent problem to be the hopelessness and despair of the people, but, he added, "You can't deal with that until you deal with all the other problems." It is not a matter of having the problems solved for the people, however. It is a matter of organizing the people themselves to effect solutions, and it is in the experiencing of this efficacy that the hopelessness and despair is spoken to. "If you find you can do something about your housing situation, for example, then it is not all hopeless."

Many groups are active in the community, but in terms of achieving power for the people, none is really effective, according to Rev. A. Some "have no structure"; others are most effective in "keeping power away from the people." The one organization which is really working at organizing the people is the East Garfield Park Community Organization (EGPCO). He illustrated its lack of tangible success, however, by noting that it got only 500 votes for the independent aldermanic candidate it supported.

Rev. A. is deeply involved in this organization. He maintains that while it has been ineffective in terms of solid accomplishments, it has been very effective in its process of working toward power: "A loss can still be a victory in the personal life of people. Poor people can't win organizational struggles; therefore the personal victory is the only victory possible. And this is more important in the long run." EGPCO's membership is by individuals rather than groups, and this has resulted in a "much closer feeling of community" among the members.

Rev. A. ranks community activity as having priority both ideally and actually, as well as giving him the most satisfaction. He gives no emphasis to the "inner life of faith and devotion" in his preaching and teaching, and much emphasis to "community responsibility" and "social issues." He has taken public stands on all of the issues that we listed in our questionnaire and participated in every kind of community activity listed.

He does not feel that he has the support of the congregation in his ministry. His original theory was that "the community organization was a way of bringing the church and community together, a kind of bridge. The congregation reacted, however, by leaving the church." He does have the support of the denomination, including finances, but not to the extent that he considers necessary.

Rev. A. has been harassed by the established political organization for his community organizing action. His church has been picketed and threatened with being closed down. Even the support of the people of the community itself is ambiguous. During the interview, a black lady came in to complain about the tactics of the EGPCO, in which "stewards" are appointed for each apartment building, with the responsibility for identifying and reporting instances of landlord negligence. This lady felt the whole problem could be solved by ghetto people keeping their own apartments clean.

Rev. A. says that EGPCO has "been more the church than the church. We serve communion at the meetings, and testify about our problems. There is prayer and hymn singing." He says that it is "crisis that unites us, and if the church is to survive it must find a uniting crisis." "The church has to become part of the world. To be free one must be for others, and to be for others, one must have the experience of another being for you." Therefore he works for better housing, a more responsive political structure, in short, "people power."

Rev. A.'s ministry is one of those which is most consistently in the public style. In both his community awareness and participation, legitimation is almost totally withheld from the given system, and sensitizing and politicizing are dominant. But in terms of the latter, he emphasizes "communal adequacy" over "organizational competence." It is interesting to conjecture whether he has not, in the process of actualizing the public style, come to have a parochial understanding of the EGPCO, exchanging one parish for another.

Rev. B. says that the community "shares in the problems of any black ghetto: housing, education, employment are all inadequate. Business and political power is exercised by outside interests who use rather than serve the community." He sees the political problem as the most comprehensive. The "cynicism of the party" and the "inability of the community to oppose the party" causes the residents to subject themselves to threats which are "not empty."

Some response is being made by the community, however, Rev. B. pointed out. Two elections ago the independent aldermanic candidate had carried only 3 of 59 precincts. In the most recent election the independent candidate, a deacon in one of the local congregations, carried 37 of 59 precincts, although he still was defeated. The candidate was supported by a number of pastors and congregations. During the election compaign Rev. B. was instrumental in forming the Ad Hoc Committee for Justice in Elections, which included 29 ministers from various parts of Chicago. The purpose was to protest the "indiscriminate disqualifying" of independent candidates by the Board of Election. The committee appeared as a group before Mayor Daley. Rev. B. and another of the pastors also testified at a state senate hearing on election reform. This is an example both of attempting to sensitize the official political process and of parallel political activity.

One of the results of the aldermanic campaign was the organizing of GO (the Garfield Organization). GO is an attempt to bring the city "honest representation" by bringing together those local community groups and interests which have similar goals. They include a number of the churches and several black militant groups.

Rev. B. was one of those who helped organize GO. His congregation is a member, and one of his deacons is a staff member. He feels that it is too early to tell how effective GO will be, but it already has several victories to point to, among them forcing a couple of retail stores to bring their prices and quality of merchandise into line. One of the goals is to organize block clubs on a precinct basis, so that a structure "parallel to the machine" with its own precinct captains can be built up, and thus be in a position to challenge the machine.

Rev. B. and his congregation are also active participants in CAM. He sees CAM as a means of building a sense of community, training leadership, and providing community services. It has provided some of the initial impetus and leadership for GO, and GO in turn can become the political arm of the community which CAM is attempting to build.

In the questionnaire, Rev. B. hesitated to rank community activity ahead of preaching and calling, but would not rank the latter ahead of community activity either. In the interview he said that he couldn't really distinguish "community activity" as a separate concern, but that certainly 80 percent of his time was spent "outside of the parochial structure." CAM receives much of that time, and he considers CAM to be a major aspect of his congregation's life.

Rev. B. has received major opposition only from the political machine, and he related its opposition primarily to his participation in GO. For the most part his "congregation is totally behind him; people relate to the church because of my style of ministry." The immediate community is "100 percent supportive." The denomination provides financial support both for the congregation and for CAM, and it is also expected to provide support for GO. The denominational executive has given "behind the scenes" support to Rev. B.

Rev. B. has participated in every kind of community action listed in our questionnaire and taken public stands on all but a couple of the public issues. One of those which he has not taken a stand on is "organized violence as a strategy for social change," which he would consider "possible if other avenues fail." In justifying the "political" nature of his ministry, he said, "The goal of the church is the full stature of every person in the community, i.e., every person reaching the potential for which he is created. This involves political action, and therefore political action is certainly a part of the work of the church, as Christ's body in the world."

Rev. B. recognizes both public and parochial responsibilities, but evidences a merging of the two responsibilities in a predominantly public style of fulfilling them. As with Rev. A., there is also perhaps an expanded sense of the parochial, including the more public structures of CAM and GO.

Rev. C. places the problems of Garfield Park in the larger context of the black community. Therefore he sees the first need to be the "formulation of racial pride and the dignity of man that comes with it." In addition he sees the need for a form of ecumenism which would have teams of ministers, not necessarily of the same denomination, working out of community churches. Finally, he mentioned the need for better schools, employment opportunities, and housing. He stated that CAM has effectively tackled the first problem with its pre-school-to-adult education program, which includes an emphasis on Negro history. CAM responds to the other two needs as well.

If GO is successful it "will provide a non-partisan political force, raise indigenous leaders, and promote Negro economic participation." He sees CAM as a "direct, prophetic expression of the Gospel," while GO is an "expression of the secular."

Rev. C. is an officer in both CAM and GO. He believes that community activity ought to rank first among the various aspects of the ministry, and it actually does receive the greatest proportion of his time. He spends about 15 percent of his time on the congregation and its program, 5 percent on what he calls "stupid work." The rest is spent with the community. On the other hand he considers CAM to be a part of the congregation's life and work. In terms of satisfaction received, he ranks community activity and preaching and teaching equally high. In his preaching and teaching he gives much emphasis to both the "inner life" and "personal relationships," and to "community responsibility" and "social issues." He has taken public stands on most of the issues and participated in each kind of community action listed in the questionnaire.

He feels that the congregation fully supports his style of ministry, except for an occasional complaint that he is "hard to catch." The congregation supports financially CAM, GO, and the Mississippi Delta Ministry. The denomination is "years behind, by far. But they let me go my way. It's strange; they like to show our congregation off, but don't approve of me personally." The denomination contributes financially both to the congregation and to CAM. The support of the general community is indicated by his being invited by a number of community groups (not including the Regular Democratic organization) to be a candidate for public office.

Rev. C. says he follows the "format of Barth" in grounding his participation in the community. "All men are elected through Christ to salvation, even though they don't act like it. One of the reasons is that we don't even know that we are elected, because we are unloved or lost, and therefore cannot respond to anything. CAM is able to free people to the extent that they can respond to their personal election." He says further that there is in the church a sense of being a part of a "kingdom which is both present and ahead," and this adds strength to its participation.

One of the fundamental assumptions of Rev. C.'s participation in the community is that the status quo cannot be legitimated. A second is that the sensitizing and politicizing functions must be fulfilled parallel to the established social and political organization. The church's mission is bound up with this need. The result is a ministry which is wholly public in style. Like Rev. B., he does not consider this style to be at the expense of parochial concerns, but as the means by which parochial concerns can best be met. An interesting footnote is that Rev. C's long range hope is not to be a holder of elected office, but a "teacher in a college or seminary."

The public style, in its most consistent form, is observed in the ministries of all three of these men. It is not just the style of their community participation, but of their whole ministry. Rev. A. appears almost to have given up his parish for the community organization. Revs. B. and C., on the other hand, have been able to understand and carry out their parish and community participation as a single ministry. There is no hesitancy on the part of any of the three to consider the politicizing function as a valid part of ministry. Legitimation is given to the people's participation in the decision-making process. This requires parallel political organization. Communal adequacy then is a part of the object of community action; organizational competence is a means. The authenticity of the church in that situation demands this style of ministry.

In addition to the situation, the presence of like-minded colleagues, congregational and community support, and appropriate structures have reinforced the sense of need for and helped to implement the public style in the ministers' community participation. Although denominational support has contributed to the ministries, the initiative in each case appears to be with the ministers in their parishes.

## Lincoln Park

Lincoln Park, a "middle" type community is located on the north side of Chicago, somewhat closer to the Loop than to the northern city limit. It extends from Lake Michigan westward to the Chicago River. The city park which gives its name to the community area is located along the lake. Just west of the park is a part of the city's "gold coast," a strip of high-rise, high-rent apartment buildings. The part of Lincoln Park which gives it the "middle" classification is between this strip and the river. All of the churches whose ministers we interviewed are in this section of the area.

The area included in Lincoln Park was settled by German and Scotch-Irish truck gardeners in the 1850's and '60's. It was not until 1889 that the entire area became a part of the city of Chicago. By then large industrial plants had moved into the area, attracting Polish as well as more German and Irish workmen as residents. By 1895, the community was residentially mature, that is, all available residential land had been built up.

The period between 1900 and 1960 was one of internal change: encroachment of industry into residential areas; greater heterogeneity of population, including some non-whites; the breaking up of large homes into rooming houses; the construction of some public housing at the northwest corner, and luxury housing adjacent to the park.

The peak population of Lincoln Park was 100,826 in 1940. In 1960, the population was down to 88,836; the estimated 1966 population was 82,631. The non-white population increased between 1960 and 1966 from 4.7 percent to an estimated 7.5 percent, and is concentrated in the southwest corner of the community. Lincoln Park experiences the problems of racial segregation at the secondary school level. It is part of Chicago District 7 which extends both north and south of the area. The northern half of District 7 is almost all white; the southwestern section is mostly black. Lincoln Park's high school is a meeting ground for the two races, but there was a move to build a new high school to the north, which would remove most white students.

In the seven indices of human welfare need used in our study, the section of Lincoln Park exclusive of the "gold coast" strip, ranked among the 30 least favorable community areas. For example, the income of over 15 percent of the families was under $3,000. The 1966 Hospital Planning Council study assigns it the economic rank of 224, out of the 250 metropolitan communities (the section along the lake is ranked 105, indicating the contrast).

Urban Renewal has brought dramatic change to Lincoln Park. A newspaper item at the time of our study quotes a resident as saying, "People are delighted; they're really proud. . . . We're inviting our friends in from the suburbs to show it all off." But there are other opinions. Another resident said, "Instead of spending all this money on beautification, they ought to spend it on housing for the poor people now being crammed into corners. People are being pushed out of here."[2]

An organization which takes a great deal of credit for the improvement in Lincoln Park is the Lincoln Park Conservation Association. Founded in 1954, the LPCA is an association of residents, businessmen, institutional representatives and neighborhood groups, including some of the churches. It is an example of a local community organization more oriented to property owners than to residents regardless of property ownership.

The LPCA makes an enthusiastic assessment of what is going on in Lincoln Park. Concerned Citizens of Lincoln Park have a less enthusiastic assessment. The latter group has been organized to obtain more low and middle income housing in the urban renewal area. Citizens United for Better Education (CUBE) is another organization which feels that the LPCA is not taking a broad enough approach to community issues.

The heterogeneity of the community is reflected in its churches: a variety of Baptist churches, including several of the black Baptist groups; pentecostal churches, including Spanish-speaking; both a Greek and a Romanian Orthodox congregation; half a dozen Roman Catholic parishes; and congregations of the denominations of our sample. The North Side Cooperative Ministry (NSCM) begun in 1963, is also a part of the church situation. It has about 25 member churches in an area of which Lincoln Park is the middle third. The NSCM is concerned with both service to the community and service to the local member congregations. The primary emphasis is on the former, however, and is implemented by a wide variety of task force groups.

In addition, a number of the Lincoln Park ministers have been meeting almost daily to discuss and plan for ministry in their own community. A member of the Chicago Presbytery staff, working within a Church Federation-sponsored cooperative urban program, has been meeting with them as a catalyst and resource person.

All of the congregations in our sample have been in the community for more than fifty years. All but one of them have adult memberships of fewer than 500--four of them fewer than 300. Only one reports a trend of increasing membership during the past five years. Reasons for decreasing membership include both a changing racial makeup of the population and general disinterest on the part of persons moving into the area.

Three of the congregations have more than 50 percent of their members over 50 years of age; only one has less than 25 percent. The socio-economic status of the memberships tends to be higher than that of the community as a whole. A few black and oriental persons are to be found among the memberships of the churches, but most congregations are all white. Two of the churches are receiving program grants from their denominations; the rest are self-supporting in their operational expenses.

Four of the eight ministers are under thirty-five years of age; two of them are over fifty-five. Five of them have been in their present congregation five years or less, and one has been in Lincoln Park over ten years. All but one live within six blocks of the church building. The members on the other hand are more scattered, although at least 50 percent of the members of most of the congregations live within a mile of the church.

What is the style of community participation of these ministers of older, somewhat declining congregations in a community of multiple problems, but also of multiple responses to the problems?

Rev. D. began his discussion of the community by saying that urban renewal was reversing the trend which until five years previously was causing Lincoln Park to "go down the drain." Now upper middle income people are moving back. But at the same time urban renewal is "on the verge of neatly arranging it so that middle to low income people can not live here." He is active in the NSCM and meets with the group of local ministers, both of which are concerned with the housing issue. He is also a member of the Community Conservation Committee, by the appointment of the Mayor. The latter committee is in a sense responsible for the circumstances which are of concern to the former.

Rev. D. says that he feels himself in tension between "good urban renewal which at times can't be kind, and the Christian clergyman's concern for people no matter what." This minister understands the need for new approaches to community participation, but is committed in responsibility to the more conventional approaches such as the Mayor's committee and serving on the boards of several institutions. This undoubtedly has been determined to a great extent by the particular congregation he serves and his relatively long tenure as its minister.

Community activity consumes at least half of his working time. He says that "as of now it takes too much time. A man can go overboard and neglect the work of keeping the congregation running. When you lose the structural church, you will lose your anchor. Therefore it is essential to keep the church healthy and growing, finding ways of bringing into the church those residents who have previously expressed no interest in it." He is more active in the community than he had been, primarily because he has become more and more convinced that "if the church is going to be the church in the world it will have to go into the community."

Rev. D. says that he does a great deal of preaching on the responsibility of the church in contemporary culture. "If the church is really the church then it is concerned for people who find it difficult to keep a roof over their head and bread on their table. If one seriously talks about God's saving work, one can't separate out housing, race relations, and Viet Nam." "At this moment I would have to say that urban renewal is a part of God's saving grace, the process by which God works in history, although this doesn't mean it is all good."

Most of his congregation approve of his style of participation; in fact they encourage it, Rev. D. said. Many of the laymen are also active in the community. The congregation is a member of the NSCM and of the LPCA. One member is on the board of the JYDC, another on the Mayor's Commission on Human Relations, one was President of the LPCA, and another is active in CUBE. A congregational study group has been discussing Viet Nam, and laymen have spoken during the Sunday morning service on subjects such as Viet Nam and gun control legislation. He feels that one of the best services the church can render society is to have its members in the policy and decision-making structures.

Rev. D. feels best equipped for a more conventional type of community participation, working through a pastoral ministry and serving in more legitimating capacities. He believes that this type of ministry is necessary, but not adequate. Therefore, he is interested in getting an associate minister who is equipped to handle the less parochial and legitimating types of activity.

Rev. E. feels that Urban Renewal is dealing mostly with propertied people, people with money invested in the community. "They don't want poor people around." And "the community organization does not represent the people either, its focus being on the business community." He sees the LPCA as merely working on the city's plans. Concerned Citizens of Lincoln Park, on the other hand, is holding up alternative plans and is calling for the city to "take more seriously the citizens of the community and their ability to decide what the community should be like."

Rev. E. is active in the latter group, but is seeking to develop a large community organization, concerned not only with housing, but also health, education, etc. He says that none of the groups dealing with housing has been successful to this point because they "haven't been able to come up with the power and resources to effect change in a highly structured urban complex." The hope for the new organization is to acquire such power and resources.

About 60 percent of Rev. E.'s time is devoted to community activity. He ranks community activity first in the relative importance it ought to have in his ministry, in the time he actually gives to it, and in the amount of satisfaction he receives from it. He has participated in every kind of community action that was listed in our questionnaire. In his preaching and teaching he gives some emphasis to the "inner-life," and much emphasis to "community responsibility" and "social issues." He has publicly expressed his support of over half the public issues listed in our questionnaire, including both the statewide open occupancy law, and the housing protest marches.

He is much more involved in the community than he was in his previous parish, a rural situation. Not, however, because there were no problems, but "because I didn't understand the problems, and when I did move, I had no strategy." His present congregation supports his style of ministry, but this is in large part due to the nature of the congregation itself. It was formed on the "thesis that this church would be involved in community issues." The denomination is "not openly supporting us or holding us up as a model, but it is not resisting us either, although I don't know how much longer we'll enjoy that situation." The congregation is a contributing member of both the NSCM and the LPCA, and is engaged corporately in many community concerns along with the minister. The weekday experiences of the congregation are incorporated in the Sunday worship. Small study groups are seeking to establish a "theological and economic understanding of culture."

The basic theological understanding of Rev. E.'s ministry is that "God works in this world and the church is called to celebrate and join in the mission which we call the 'humanizing process.'" The church then is "basically a social force, responding to human needs where it sees them, both bandaging the wounds and arresting the problems that cause the wounds. This means getting involved in changing the political system." The new organizing effort is to develop "a vision of how God's creation can be made most beneficial to human beings, of how man might reach his full potential in twentieth century urban life." Rev. E. adds, however, that "because of the sin and self-interest of the church," it may be doing the wrong thing in any given project. Nevertheless this is the work it must be about.

Rev. F. is also concerned with what Urban Renewal is doing to the diversity of the community, and he does not think any group has been particularly effective in dealing with the problem. He thinks that the LPCA and other neighborhood associations "have fallen into the hands of those who don't want the community to be diverse, speculators who are more interested in young adults than families." Concerned Citizens "tends to be a little doctrinaire," but it is an attempt in the right direction, "trying to draw priorities of price ranges instead of only time tables for building." Personally, he is inclined toward the position that the best strategy would be to bring urban renewal to a vote, "get out enough 'no' votes, and then negotiate."

The bulk of Rev. F.'s time is spent in "trying to discover the nature of the pathology of this congregation." The congregation has suffered considerable membership and financial loss, but while he feels that this losing trend has been halted now, he also feels that there is much to be done in developing a "concept of church membership and responsibility." He would like to develop a "federation of groups" of diverse backgrounds and points of view and styles of life, rather than a "homogeneous congregation in the old style." This involves holding off an attempt of the "old guard to prevent people from 'being themselves.'"

The congregation as a whole is not involved in the community. The social ministry committee, however, is concerned with community organization and encouraging membership involvement. There is also a youth program which attempts to serve the community. Rev. F. is considering an organization of the congregation which would have interests and concerns parallel to those of the community organization, so that the congregation would be structurally prepared to work with the community.

Rev. F. says that he is about equally involved in the community as in his previous parish, although here it is a more "'secular' involvement, as a private citizen rather than as an institutional leader, as previously." Community activity receives about 20 percent of his time, and he ranks it second both in ideal and actual priority. His personal involvement centers on the schools. He is a member of the Schools Committee of the local neighborhood affiliate of the LPCA. He sees this as a "propagandizing" effort for the public school, which in turn can attract and maintain families of school age children. Many of the parents in the neighborhood can afford to send their children to private schools, taking away parent support from the public school. Rev. F. is particularly interested in families for the community because he believes that they are more responsible to the community as "a place of living--of friends and activities," while single young adults and childless couples are interested only in "high-rise shelter and safety."

Rev. F. interprets his concern to bring the congregation into relation with the community as a way of demonstrating that "all people are God's people and therefore they have a certain value and need to be freed up to find their humanity. One of the ways of witnessing is standing up for the rights of people as human beings. The real crisis of our day is the refusal of humanity. The need of today is to reshape society so it is possible to be human, which is what it means to live as a saved man." Among other things this involves a "new style of service, that is, not giving food to the hungry, but finding out why they are hungry in the first place, and this means getting involved in the system to find out why."

Rev. F. appears to be seeking to move his congregation to a public style of ministry. His strategy is to begin with the parochial situation as far as the congregation as a whole is concerned and to move ahead as an individual in the public arena. He is sensitive to personal risk in the process, specifically the risk of loss of favor with the denomination, and the support of the congregation. And it is only when a minister "makes up his mind that he can always sell shoes that he becomes free enough to take the risk."

The ministry of Lincoln Park manifests a public style, in participation in community life. Many factors seem to be involved in the development of this style. Not only the deteriorating conditions of the community, but the city's determination to renew the community are involved. A strong community organization provided precedent and impetus for other community strategies. A broad ecumenical association likewise provided precedent and impetus for a more specifically local ecumenical association.

The working out of the public style is not the same for all ministers. Nevertheless, there is strong evidence, both in the acting out and the articulation of the public style, that most of the ministers have worked and reflected together. Although each of the ministers has his particular participation, none gives the impression of feeling alone in what he is doing, but rather of enjoying the stimulation and support of his colleagues.

## South Holland

The "low" community for which we shall describe the profile of participation is South Holland, a suburb just south of the city limits of Chicago. For the first 100 years of its existence (until about 1950), South Holland was a settlement of persons of Dutch origin, with farming as the chief occupation. In 1950, the population of the village was 3,247. Two-thirds of the foreign-born population came from the Netherlands. Only 18 percent of the working population was classified as management and professional. By 1960, the population had increased to 10,412. Persons born in the Netherlands made up only one-third of the foreign-born (although it was still the country of origin of the largest number of foreign-born, by far). Workers in the management and professional classification made up 40 percent of the working population.

The estimated population in 1966 was 17,030, over five times that of 1950. One of the ministers of the village estimated that in 1950 the community was 95 percent Dutch Reformed, but that in 1967 it was about 50 percent Roman Catholic and only 30 percent Dutch Reformed. Yet despite the increase in population and the change of composition of the population, South Holland apparently has not changed much as a place to live.[3]

An historian of the village writes that the community leadership is still Dutch Reformed (in 1966). Four of the seven members of the village board are members of Reformed congregations. In addition the "cultural" climate remains the same. "For the most part the newcomer chose South Holland as his place of residence for the very reason that he sometimes jokingly upbraids his Dutch neighbor--no taverns, no Sunday business, no apartments--in general, an excellent environment in which he can raise his children."[4]

South Holland is thus family and home-oriented. It is middle class, with the family having an average income of $8,300, and the home having an average value of $19,778. And it is white. In 1960, 16 (0.2 percent) of the 10,412 persons were non-white; in 1966, 17 (0.1 percent) of the 17,030 persons were non-white. Not only are the people of South Holland white, but they are white people many of whom have left the city of Chicago in the face of the expansion of the black ghetto. One minister said that, "Most people here moved out of the city and I would judge that more than 50 percent were people fleeing the Negro."

One of the ironies of the situation, however, is that South Holland is in a school district which includes two other suburbs with large black populations (about 5,000 each). A community "event" mentioned in each of the interviews was the defeat of a school bond election twice in the preceding twelve months. The purpose of the bonds was to build a third high school, which would have changed the racial pattern from one all-white and one integrated high school to three integrated high schools. The defeat of the election was attributed to the desire of whites to avoid integration. (Subsequently the school district has become the object of the federal government's first suit on de facto segregation brought against a northern school district.)

The ministers generally agree that youth gangs, deteriorating housing, inadequate public education, and police harassment are not problems in South Holland. Family instability is considered to be somewhat of a problem by three of the ministers, and mental and emotional stress by four of them. Racial prejudice is the only one of the problems listed in the questionnaire considered to be serious; three of the ministers list it as serious, and two as only somewhat a problem. Four of the five ministers rate their community as above average as a place to live compared with other sections of the Chicago metropolitan area.

Three of the congregations of these five ministers are less than ten years old; one is over fifty. None are engaged in building programs, but all are paying off mortgages of previous building programs. Less than 25 percent of the adult membership in each of the congregations is over fifty years of age. All of the ministers reported a trend of increasing membership, due mainly to a gain in community population, but also due to the church program, and general interest of newcomers in church participation. Only one of the congregations receives financial aid from its denomination or other outside source. Within the memberships of the five congregations there is one black family.

South Holland itself has a ministerial association, dominated by the Dutch Reformed ministers. The ministerial association drawing from two neighboring communities is also open to South Holland ministers. Two groups are active in relation to the race problem, a human relations committee, and a voluntary group concerned specifically with housing.

What is the style of community participation of ministers in this kind of a community and church setting?

Rev. G. reflects the positive evaluation of the community in saying, "Other than the fact that there are no Negroes, there are no community problems." He considers racial prejudice to be only somewhat of a problem, and does not see Negro move-ins as much of a threat because of the price range of the housing. "I think the community does not want integrated schooling," he said.

He does not participate in nor is he aware of any local organizations dealing with the racial problem. He considers the local ministerial association, of which he is a member, as not being primarily concerned with community problems, although they discuss them when they arise. Rev. G. gives only some emphasis to "members' responsibility in community life" in his preaching and teaching, and little emphasis to the "large social issues of the day." Community activity ranks last among the various aspects of his ministry in time spent, although he feels it "ought" to come ahead of administrative work.

He feels that he might be more involved in the community in a different situation: "Because of the nature of this community there are no real welfare problems." Nevertheless, the tradition of his denomination tends to cause its ministers to be "very isolated in this sense, to be non-involved. Working in the community is valid too, but in order of importance ministry through Word and sacrament comes first." He has participated in none of the types of action listed in our questionnaire. He has taken public stands only in support of the neighborhood school policy and against the strategy of violence.

Rev. G. manifests a consistently parochial style of ministry. His perception of the state of the community and his general motivation are appropriate to that style. He acknowledges the parochial style in his ministry, but appears to be quite comfortable with it.

Rev. H. considers prejudice to be the major problem of that community and the surrounding communities as well. In addition South Holland is an "intolerable place in terms of the conservative religious climate--politically too." The prejudice is caused by a "fear of having to endure the same experience as they had in Chicago, loss of property values, etc." He thinks, however, that the city itself is seen as a threat. In a congregational questionnaire, "Seventy percent of the people thought the congregation should be involved in seeking constructive solutions to the problem of race; but 70 percent thought they should <u>not</u> become involved in a Chicago inner city project."

The human relations committee has been ineffective in dealing with the problem of race: "They just meet and talk and soothe each other's conscience with words." He sees no real hope coming out of it, and therefore is not active in it. He is a member of the group working on housing and is active in the inter-community ministerial association, but does not consider either of them to be effectively dealing with the problem. His own congregation, however, has a committee which is attempting to deal with the issue, and is moving toward working with a neighboring Roman Catholic congregation.

When Rev. H. says "I have no real community involvement," this evidently refers to active involvement in ongoing community membership action organizations. He says that community activity ranks fourth out of the four aspects of his ministry (although it ought to rank second), but it absorbs 20 to 25 percent of his time. Much of this time is spent in working with his own people and his own structure, the Committee on Community Life. There are a number of community leaders among the congregation's membership, and he is in frequent contact with them. He gives some emphasis to "members' responsibility in community life" in his preaching and teaching and much emphasis to the "large social issues of the day."

Rev. H. finds himself more active in the community than previously, not because he is more active in community organizations, but because his congregation is such as to enable him to deal with community issues within the congregation. This does not mean that all of the members agree with him. "Many members are very much opposed to the denomination's stand on housing and welfare." Nevertheless, neither he nor those members who do support such stands are afraid to speak out. He has spoken in support both of open occupancy legislation and housing protest marches, but also in support of the neighborhood school policy. He is going to ask the local congregation's board to take some stands on social issues, which they have previously not done.

In contrast to Rev. G., Rev. H. finds his own denominational tradition encouraging the church's involvement in community affairs. He has assumed this, but if he had to articulate the reason why, it would be that "the church stands for and proclaims the uniqueness and sacredness of individuals. The implication of this is, among other things, that a man has a right to live where he chooses and can afford. If God is active in history, one of the ways we see his activity is in the concrete situation, the civil rights movement. The church must actively work to make the community free of prejudice. Racial prejudice is sin; it keeps men from becoming what they are meant to be. And those who are prejudiced must be saved from their prejudice." In his ministry he tries to "create a partial understanding of some of the problems of society, and in some cases a different understanding of the church in relation to those problems." It is the difference between being an "individual club," and being "responsible to the community as a whole."

Rev. H. exemplifies the public style of participation of ministry--in awareness, motivation, and action. The exception to this would be that he works primarily through his congregation. But this is due to two circumstances: first he feels he is able to act effectively through his congregation; second, there are no viable non-congregational structures available. Furthermore, Rev. H. said that he, along with some others, is working for the establishment of a "viable community organization," which will be concerned with human relations, although "not exclusively so." Thus he is aware of and is taking steps toward establishing a structure for effective politicizing activity, in addition to the sensitizing activity in which he already is much involved.

Rev. I. stated that the "outstanding problem is that of integration, i.e., that there is none." He believes that it is "something that ought to take place and that it is going to be a painful experience when it does." He admits that his own congregation is a result of the larger number of people who have "run" from Chicago. Yet he feels that they have not all moved because they wanted to, that in many cases they have been "harassed out." Integration should take place as a "natural thing, for example, a Negro family who fits in should have the opportunity to move in if they want to." Rev. I. is opposed to housing demonstrations in white neighborhoods.

He is concerned that no one in the community is really working on the problem. The human relations committee is "more of a paper organization than anything." The general attitude in South Holland is "We'll get to it when it happens." Rev. I. feels there should be a program of education to accept change with as little disturbance as possible. There is "no concerned leadership of strength that can spearhead a preparatory program." Attempts to discuss it in the local ministerial association have gotten nowhere.

The only way he has been able to involve himself in dealing with community issues is through the ministerial association. But, he says, "I feel overwhelmed by my Reformed colleagues. Anything on an ecumenical basis is purely a matter of coincidence, since the Reformed clergymen call the shots. We operate as a minority in this community. The two Lutheran ministers and I are continually reminded of this."

Rev. I. gives the greatest proportion of his time to administration, and the least to community activity. He is satisfied with the latter's position, although not the former's. In his preaching and teaching he gives some emphasis both to "members' community responsibility" and the "large social issues of the day." Some of his members say the "minister has no business in politics, within which they include social issues although they would be for my taking a stand on something like a Sunday closing ordinance." He has taken a public stand in support of open occupancy legislation; although he is opposed to housing protest marches, he has not stated so publicly. He has, however, publicly stated his support of the neighborhood school policy.

His congregation's community action is limited to sponsoring a kindergarten and providing facilities for a program for the mentally retarded. The official board of the congregation considers inappropriate such action as sending a letter pertaining to community matters to the village board. Because of the divergence of opinion in the congregation, Rev. I. thinks this is just as well. In general, he feels that he and his congregation are "perhaps not as advanced as his denomination in terms of social issues."

Concern for and action in the community is a matter of the "practical application of the Christian Gospel. Man must be reconciled to man, but this cannot take place if man is not first reconciled to God." Rev. I. feels that much of Christian social action violates this priority. "I think we get all enthused, involved in a lot of social action projects, without first being clear about the Christian faith and Christian doctrine. What I believe about God and man must precede what I do or go along with. Motivation must come from worship. Therefore the sanctuary predominates the church plan here."

The most significant thing in his ministry during the past year had been a Bible study program in which about fifty of his own members together with members of two other churches of his denomination participated. As a result he feels his "people are searching, trying to understand what the Christian faith really is, what the New Testament is really saying to our times. While nothing objective has happened in the way of action, there is evidence of some changed minds or opinions."

Rev. I. is one of those whose ministry fits the criteria of the "most consistent" parochial type. He is aware of problems in the community, and feels that he and his congregation have a responsibility to respond to them. But he is torn between the need for some kind of initiative and the desire to let things take their course, both in the community and the congregation. He senses the need for some kind of community structure outside the congregation, but is not ready himself to assume leadership in organizing such a structure.

In South Holland the ministers to whom we spoke are aware of a situation to which the parochial style of participation is not entirely adequate, but the public style has not emerged as an alternative, except for one of them. One would assume that were some kind of community structure for dealing effectively with community issues to be established, the ministers would be ready to give some time to it. But the priorities of the ministers are such that only one is considering giving time to initiating such a structure. The rest have plenty to keep them busy in the meantime. The problems do not interfere that much with their day-to-day ministry.

There is a common body of information concerning the community which comes through in the interviews. On the other hand, there is a great deal of diversity in opinions and evaluations expressed in the questionnaires. There is no evidence of a common thinking through of the issue of racial prejudice, for example, and certainly no evidence of arriving at a common strategy. On the whole, the ministers operate independently of one another, conducting their own programs in their own style.

## Summary

The most striking contrast in the profiles in the three types of communities is that of the participation of the ministers in the "low" community with the participation of the ministers in the other two communities. The differentiating factors are many: the presence or absence of pressing community issues, particularly those immediately hurtful to members of the community, the presence or absence of community structures for participation, the presence or absence of a working relation among the ministers, the greater or less press of parochial administrative work, the amount of progress in analyzing the social situation, and thinking through alternatives for action.

The difference between the ministers of the "high" and "middle" communities appears to be more one of degree than kind. Ministers of the "high" community spend more time in the community; on the other hand ministers of the "middle" community have a greater variety of and more advanced structures of participation. A partial explanation is found in the greater community resources immediately available in the "middle" community.

Again we note that these communities were not selected as necessarily being typical, but because they include the varieties of church and community situations and styles of ministry to which we have referred in previous chapters. These profiles serve as additional background for the concluding considerations in the chapter which follows.

## CHAPTER V

## REVIEW AND REFLECTIONS

The presence of the public style in a sizable sample of ministers, in a cross-section of types of communities, in a significant urban area, has been demonstrated in the preceding chapters. An observable relationship between the degree and content of the public style and the type of community has also been demonstrated. In its concrete, observable aspects, then, the relationship between the local community and the local community congregation has been established and described, to the extent that it is represented by its minister. The persistence of this style in time and its extent in space can be determined only by additional research. This chapter reviews the more theoretical aspects of the study and reflects upon the study in terms of its implications for the church and its ministry.

### Review of the Sociological Background

Chapter I characterized the larger social situation within which contemporary churches exist and carry out their mission with the concept of "urbanization." Urbanization emphasizes change as the dominant social condition, man as the dominant social agent, and control of change in behalf of human well-being as the dominant social need.

"Urbanization" is not a word which is universally used by ministers to describe the situation in which they minister. On the other hand the condition which it describes, particularly that of "change," is something with which the ministers are quite familiar. Regardless of the significance which they attach to it for their own work, the ministers are aware that the social situation within which they minister is a new one. Things are just not the same.

There is a difference in how the new situation is described, however. Some ministers see the change as primarily quantitative: more people, more problems, less responsibility, declining support, etc. Evaluation is in terms of "better" or "worse" than before. Some ministers see the change as primarily qualitative: new kinds of people, different problems, new possibilities, alternative values, etc. Evaluation is in terms of "good" or "bad," "acceptable" or "unacceptable."

There is also a difference in what are considered to be the causes. Most ministers understand man as the dominant social agent, and control of change in behalf of human well-being as the dominant social need. But some of the ministers see the breakdown in man's agency as one of neglect.

Man is on the whole well-intentioned, but he has let things get out of control. Other ministers see the breakdown of man's agency as one of intent. Those in a position to do so have intentionally used their positions to enhance their own position at the expense of the powerless. The forces of urbanization have given them powerful new opportunities and resources to consolidate and expand their power.

Chapter I also proposed the concept of the "self-transforming society" as a sociological framework for response to the need for social control. The self-transforming society is one which is able to control the forces at work within society, including the forces of urbanization, for the well-being of its citizenry. The key to social transformation, we concluded, "is that of a realistic, rational, and responsible process of social policy formation and implementation." The focal point is the politicizing function; the goal is that it be orderly and intentional, realistic in its grasp of the societal situation, and responsible to the needs and desires of those affected by decision and action. Thus the politicizing function must be complemented by the sensitizing and legitimating functions.

The concept of a "self-transforming" society itself would not be immediately meaningful to the thinking of many of the ministers. They do not think in terms of a transformed society. A few of them would probably tend to think in terms of a "self-maintaining society." Most would probably be more comfortable with the concept of a "self-correcting" society, a society which is able to make the necessary changes to achieve those values which have been accepted from the beginning, and continue to be valid. The "self-transforming" society concept includes the possibility that the values themselves may have to be changed, and fewer ministers are thinking in these terms.

The particular concept conditions how the functions of sensitizing, politicizing, and legitimating are understood. Most ministers become socially aware at the level of the legitimating function, that is, where the needs and desires of the public are considered, most particularly that portion of the public residing within their parish boundaries. Ministers are expected to contribute to the legitimating function, but find that in view of conditions for living in their local communities, they cannot in good conscience uncritically fulfill that function.

If the minister has assumed that those in charge will normally want to function for the well-being of the public, his next awareness will be at the politicizing level, where the decisions which affect the local community are made and implemented. The minister calls attention to community conditions, expecting that action will be taken. When no action is forthcoming, he moves to the sensitizing function. He still assumes that those in charge at the politicizing level will act, but now the problem is seen as one of coming to understand the forces contributing to the conditions and of interpreting this to those in charge.

Our survey indicates that most ministers have themselves become sensitive, in varying degrees, to underlying causes as well as conditions. The communication of sensitivity also varies, some ministers communicating primarily with members of the congregations, others directly with those in charge. The experience in the latter process has caused many of the ministers to move to the level of the politicizing function. They have found that those officially fulfilling the politicizing function are not willing or able to act in behalf of the local communities. Therefore it is necessary for the communities themselves to organize for action. The ministers' sensitivity combined with their availability and leadership capacities have made them logical initiators of and participants in the organizing process. In a sense then many of the ministers can be said to have been "politicized" by the demands of the situations in which they minister, combined with the unwillingness or inability of those who normally would be expected to act to do so.

As the people of the community are the beginning point for the minister's participation in the community, they are also the point to which he returns. He chooses his own issue and structure of participation primarily on the basis of their being worthy of legitimation to the people of the community. Having done so, he is then able to fulfill the legitimating function. His ability to do so has developed not by closing his eyes to the inadequacy of the given politicizing function, nor by his success in changing it, but rather by his discovering, perhaps organizing, an alternative politicizing structure.

While the image of the "self-transforming society" itself may not be immediately meaningful to most ministers, those functions which contribute toward it provide useful categories for interpreting the thinking and action of many of the ministers. The understanding of the politicizing function together with the evaluation of those officially fulfilling it seem to be especially critical for the kinds of responses of the ministers.

## Review of the Theological Background

"Loyalty to the kingdom of God" was proposed as a valid theme for understanding the historical participation of the Protestant churches in American social conditions and needs. Like "urbanization," and "the self-transforming society," "loyalty to the kingdom of God" is not a term that is explicitly used with great frequency by the ministers. Rather it functions as a concept within which to interpret what the ministers are saying and doing. Some ministers did speak of their participation in the context of the "kingdom." Most, however, used words like "obedience," "service," "love," "freedom," and "fulfillment." Yet these are words which are part of the vocabulary of the kingdom of God. One might say that it is the kingdom that the ministers are talking about, and that it is loyalty to the kingdom with which they are concerned. Two exceptions would be where the minister disassociates the kingdom from society, or disassociates his participation in society from his participation in the kingdom. These exceptions are rare among our sample. The image of the kingdom of God does appear to have continued relevance in understanding the participation of the Protestant churches in American social conditions and needs. Certainly it continued to be a part of the theologizing of the 1960's (cf. H. W. Richardson, <u>Toward an American Theology</u>, 1967, and James Cone, <u>Black Theology and Black Power</u>, 1969).

The main question posed for our survey, however, is concerned with the articulation of the kingdom implicit in the participation of the ministers in their communities. On the basis of the research we would draw the following summary conclusion: the presupposition of loyalty to the kingdom is "the sovereignty of God"; the primary informing image is "the reign of Christ"; "the kingdom on earth" has become the dominant informing image for those ministers who demonstrate the public style, and is implicit in the participation of many others.

The articulation of loyalty to the kingdom as the "sovereignty of God" is presupposed in two ways. It is an accepted notion that American society has not rejected its official intention (value commitment) to be a society "under God." The evaluation of America's faithfulness to that commitment varies a great deal among the ministers, but they feel that they can and must appeal to this commitment as a basis for response to the needs of human well-being. Secondly the ministers themselves accept the premise that society is subject to the sovereignty of God. Our sample of ministers is not radical in the sense of having rejected or suspended the meaningfulness of "God" and "his sovereignty."

There is no evidence of social "imperialism" among the ministers, that is, the perversion of the articulation of the sovereignty of God into a claim that American society is the embodiment and bearer of that sovereignty. While for half the ministers there is at least a tendency to feel that no other society has come closer to this than America, there is no blanket legitimation of American society as it now is. The affirmation is indeed a "restless" one at best.

The most prevalent informing articulation of the kingdom is the "reign of Christ." Social participation is a matter of "Christ's people doing Christ's work." There was little of the extreme emotionalism or individualism that in the past has been a perversion of this articulation. A mixed response to the "Billy Graham Crusade" as a social strategy is evidence of this. Of course, our denominational sample excluded those churches in which we would be most likely to encounter those emphases. What we did find was a confidence on the part of some ministers that a commitment to Christ is the primary prerequisite for effective social participation. The Christian will know what is right and will do it. If he is not doing it, it is because his commitment is inadequate.

Other ministers, while affirming the necessity of individual commitment to Christ, find it essential also to be specific about what that commitment means in actual social participation. The one in whom Christ reigns is one who loves his brother, and demonstrates this in specific kinds of actions in the particular community. Sometimes the minister has found it necessary to illustrate what it means in his own participation, or to help to organize structures through which members of the congregation can do that which is necessary. The articulation, therefore, of the "reign of Christ" can lead to an emphasis either on the commitment to Christ, or the living out of that commitment.

The articulation of loyalty to the kingdom as the "kingdom on earth" is found among those ministers for whom the criterion for the presence of the kingdom is the quality of the social life as a whole. For them the kingdom finally pays off only in terms of human social well-being--not individual people living obedient and loving lives, but communities in which a good life is experienced by those who live there. Contributing to the good life is instrumental to, not indicative of the presence of the kingdom.

This articulation of the kingdom can be perverted also, either by proclaiming that the kingdom is present in its fullness, thus "baptizing" the social situation, e.g., urbanization, or in disassociating the coming of the kingdom from the reign of Christ. The former is potentially present where ministers have plunged wholeheartedly into a particular program. But even where this is the case, the ministers seem aware of the possibilities of better or at least alternate ways of response. The latter is potentially present in the disillusionment that some ministers have experienced with those who claim to be within the reign of Christ, and the contrasting inspiration they have received from those who make no such claims.

We suggested also that the "kingdom on earth" is implicit in the participation of many ministers for whom the "reign of Christ" is the more conscious articulation. We say this because as the minister more consciously supports and encourages specific kinds of participation and is critical of specific lacks or inadequacies in the situation, he is asserting a concept of what ought to be, here and now, that is, the kingdom on earth.

What is not present, even among those ministers for whom the kingdom on earth is the informing image, is an inclusive vision of the kingdom on earth, in structural terms. The kingdom functions among most ministers on a neighborhood or local community scale. This is probably because that is where the urgency rests as well as where the ministers are. Nevertheless, it would seem that in order to use power realistically and responsibly there needs to be some concept of what the larger city would have to be for the kingdom to be present in the local community, and what would be the best arrangements for managing public resources and manufacturin and distributing the necessities and luxuries of living. It was evident that ministers do not trust the "good intentions" of either the experts, those in power, or the general public. Nevertheless the larger social unit apparently is not a major consideration for many ministers.

This "localism" perhaps can be attributed to the thrust of our research. Certainly it was focused on the problems and responses of the local community. Yet it is also true that few ministers were participating in community agencies larger in scope of concern than the local community. It should be added, however, that such agencies as the Church Federation and Urban Training Center are dealing with the kingdom on a more inclusive scale. Thus the parish minister's concentration on the local scene can be seen as a kind of specialization, with the expectation that other ministers and agencies are specializing in complementary areas.

Finally it was proposed that the "public style" characterizes an expression of professional ministry appropriate to loyalty to the kingdom of God, in the context of urbanization and the self-transforming society. It is in the style of participation in the life of the community that all of the previous ideas are expressed operationally. As we have concluded, the majority of ministers in our sample tended to validate the expectation concerning the style of participation. They are primarily institutional leaders, whose leadership has assumed a public style in relation to that part of their leadership which is directly concerned with the community of which the parish is a part. The public style is a dimension of their ministry, observable to varying degrees.

These ministers seem to have been conditioned through training and previous experience to view the problems of urbanization as problems which have always been a part of society, although not to the present extent, and that the breakdown in man's agency is mainly a matter of neglect. Nevertheless, recent reading, discussion, and especially recent experience have caused them to re-examine their analysis, to consider the possibility of qualitative change in society, and to see a barrier to change, not only in neglect but in the breakdown of intent.

They would be most apt also to think, as we have noted, in terms of a self-correcting society; but as they become aware of the kinds of corrections necessary and methods required, their thinking includes aspects of the self-transforming society. Their participation moves from the sensitizing function to participation in the politicizing function as well.

Theologically, they are most comfortable with the articulation of loyalty to the kingdom as the "reign of Christ," moving strongly toward emphasizing the living out of this reign in everyday life. And as they become more specific about the content and process of this "living out," the implications which are more reflective of "the kingdom on earth" are observable.

It appears that as the ministers become more concerned with the community, they move from familiar interpretations to less familiar, and the public style of participation becomes more apparent. Up to a point, that is. Where this participation causes him to lose his relationship with his congregation, the minister for whom the core of ministry is parochial in nature often re-evaluates his participation, and at least modifies it in order to give greater attention to the parochial concerns. The intent, however, is not to remove himself from community participation, but to strengthen the results through greater congregational participation.

There are two other groups of ministers in our sample, however, who are not accounted for by our hypothesis. These are the two groups identified in the last section of Chapter III, who most consistently express the parochial and public styles. The parochial orientation of the one group is so strong as to exclude participation in the life of the community other than that which can be accommodated within the institutional life of the congregation. Their style of ministry is parochial in its entirety. The public style is not present, even as a dimension.

These ministers tend to see the problems of urbanization to be the same problems as before, though perhaps more concentrated in particular areas, and almost entirely the result of man's neglect, to the extent that his agency is involved. Society's problem is understood mainly in terms of maintaining itself, with an acknowledgment that some correction is in order. They articulate loyalty to the kingdom almost exclusively in terms of the "reign of Christ," the emphasis being placed on commitment to Christ rather than the living out of that commitment. It is not, however, that they consider the latter irrelevant; rather they assume that if the former is present, the latter will follow. This theological understanding is accompanied by a political understanding which stresses the separation of church (in which commitment is the concern) and state (the arena of living out that commitment).

The other group is made up of those ministers whose ministry as a whole is characterized by the public style. It is in this group that the "radical view" in our sample would be found if it is present at all. And the "radical view" is in the understanding and implementation of the relation between the church and its ministry and the social situation. The social situation defines not just the style of community participation, but the entire ministry. This does not mean that the "mission" itself is devoid of theological shaping. Rather it is their theology, a predominantly "kingdom on earth" theology, which moves these ministers to a sensitivity to the needs and demands of the social situation.

The "kingdom on earth" theology is accompanied by a social analysis which sees the problems of urbanization as presenting an entirely new situation for ministry, and the breakdown in man's agency as primarily one of intent, rather than neglect. They see society as being in the process of transformation, and the social need as controlling that transformation for the well-being of man. Well-being is defined primarily in terms of fulfillment, in which freedom is the key ingredient.

The place of the congregation is not the same for this group. Some of these ministers are very parish-oriented and see the public style as that style which best fulfills the parochial responsibility, as well as the public concern. For others, the parish is mainly the operational base for their being in the particular place, but its institutional needs may run counter to and thus take second place to community participation. It is not clear whether this constitutes an abandonment of the parish idea, or a relocation of the parish in the group of community participants. (Is there here a reflection of the "camp meeting" strategy, where the expansion of the "reign of Christ" is effected outside the congregational structure, in this case in the streets, rather than in the fields?)

In any case we have already pointed out that we have no evidence among our sample that the kingdom on earth is being disassociated from the "reign of Christ," any more than from the "sovereignty of God." In several cases there is evidence, however, of its being disassociated from the local community congregation, and in more cases of its being extended beyond the congregation. There are also reflections of the Social Gospel movement here, where the kingdom is come in the structures of society. A difference, however, is that the structures where the kingdom is seen are not the structures of business and government as in the Social Gospel, but the structures of grass roots community participation. Thus there might also be said to be a re-location of the kingdom on earth, as well as the reign of Christ. The structures of business and government are not where one looks for the kingdom, but must be controlled as instruments for bringing the kingdom to the community.

Along with the continued validity of the theme of "loyalty to the kingdom," we will assert the appropriateness of the "public style" in relation to that theme. The appropriateness of this style to individual ministers, however, depends in part on their interpretation of "loyalty," and in part on their understanding of urbanization and the kinds of responses that will constructively affect it. There is both a sociological and a theological dimension to the understanding and practice of the particular style of community participation.

## FURTHER IMPLICATIONS

### A Typology of Churches

As a way of drawing things together, we may categorize concepts of the church according to the understanding of the relation of the church to society, the role of the minister, which definition of social need is accepted, and the content of the kingdom of God, to the extent that it is an "on earth" reality. There are three concepts of the church in our sample, and they correspond with the three groups of ministers referred to in the preceding section.

The first concept of the church is that of the "contributing church." The church contributes to the orderly carrying out of the life of society by producing loyal and conscientious citizens. This contribution is made, not with special programs for citizenship, but by the churches faithfully carrying out their own program of preaching and teaching the Christian faith. There is a confidence both in the power of the preaching and teaching process, and in the legitimacy of society in relation to that faith.

The content of preaching and teaching is determined by the churches. To the extent that society conditions the content, it is society embodied by the official social organization, particularly the authorized government. This does not mean that the word of government is accepted uncritically; but among the many social voices, the voice of government is most reliable, by charter and demonstrated qualification. Responsible citizenship is conceived of primarily in terms of voting, obeying the law, productive employment, and being a good neighbor.

The marks of the kingdom of God, to the extent that it can be present in society, are faithful churches (duly established congregations of people) and committed members faithfully performing their roles as citizens. The role of the minister, in the church's contribution to society is as "instructor" (sociologically, "socializer"). He does not instruct so much in the specifics of good citizenship, as in the things that motivate and prepare for good citizenship. He may declare what scripture has to say on a particular social issue, or decline to do so on the basis of there being no clear scriptural word. This concept of the church and the ministry appears to be embodied in the ministers of the most consistent parochial style, the parochial/parochial type.

According to Sidney Mead's analysis this would be an example of the logical extension of the "American experience," the church making its contribution to the nation and the nation reciprocating by allowing and encouraging the churches' presence in society. The model of the church as contributor to society can be criticized within the context of loyalty to the kingdom on one of two bases. Either it implies an over-estimation of the intention and ability of organized society to operate according to the best interests of the "kingdom," or it implies an under-estimation of the need to inform member-citizens as to specific needs and strategies for effecting control in the best interests of the "kingdom." Another way of putting it would be to say there is either too low an expectation of the possibilities for the "kingdom on earth," or too high an expectation of its inevitability.

The second concept of the church, with which the participation of most ministers (the parochial/public type) is consistent, is that of the "serving church." The church serves society by ministering to the human needs which it identifies within society. The traditional instrumentalities for such service have been, on the one hand, the social welfare institutions maintained by the churches, and the "helping hand" extended by individual members to their neighbors, on the other. In our Chicago sample, the community organization is an additional instrument. The community organization gives more concentrated attention to the local community than the congregation can, and at the same time provides the benefit of an organized approach not present in individual "helping hands."

Society's needs are defined by the persons manifesting the needs; the hungry, the poorly-housed, the unemployed. These persons are literally the "neighbor" to be served out of Christian love. There is the belief that those persons closest to the need, especially those directly experiencing the need, are better able to define the need for service than welfare agencies or city planning offices. As we move toward the extreme "public style" end of our continuum, there is a more radical rejection of the official voice in favor of the voice of the neighbor himself, and a more radical affirmation of the need for power in addition to the more traditionally legitimated needs.

The marks of the kingdom, to the extent that it is realized on earth, are loving, helping persons, and effective attention to needs. The latter mark is one of the decisive differences between the contributing and serving church. The former puts the emphasis on the contribution being made, the latter on the effectiveness of the service. In other words it is not enough that there are people trying. The expectation is that the results of that trying are seen and experienced.

The role of the minister in the serving church is that of "sensitizer" to service. He sensitizes the members of the congregation both to the essential position of service in the Christian life, and to the specific needs and resources for service in the community. He may address himself directly to the larger community as well, although the claim upon the response of the larger community cannot be the same as the claim upon members of the congregation. The clear word of scripture on neighbor love, service to the brother in need, and righteousness and justice, justify his speaking out on issues which in their particularity may not have a clear word.

This concept of the church in society is within the logical extension of the "American experience" when it allows established society to define needs and legitimate methods of meeting those needs. As such it is subject to the same criticism leveled at the concept of the "contributing church," although perhaps to a lesser degree. It is a more authentic expression of loyalty to the kingdom, and the intention of the "American experience," when it claims for itself a share in the sensitizing role, thereby opening itself for hearing the voice of the neighbor and letting its own voice be heard within the councils of those in charge.

The weakness of this approach is the tendency to concentrate on the most dramatically visible needs, the slum situation for example, and to conceive of service primarily in terms of eliminating the need. Too much emphasis is given to the physical "appearances" of human well-being; too little emphasis is given to the underlying structures and long-range possibilities of human well-being. There is a suggestion in this concept that the kingdom is indeed here; the problem is merely to bring the neglected persons and places up to standard. This ignores the sense of crisis in the coming kingdom, and the continuing necessity of probing beneath the surface in those places and persons where the kingdom appears to have come in its fullness. The Word is preached, and food, housing, and employment are adequate, but unloving attitudes and broken interpersonal relationships are equally abundant.

The third concept of the church is that of the "participating church." The church participates in the life of society. "Participating" describes the <u>membership</u> of the church--the church as institution and people as members of the community, sharing the same needs and responsibilities as other community institutions and people. "Participating" also describes the <u>task</u> of the church, to work for constructive building of community, with the full range of community resources and structures as potential instrumentalities.

The primary social point of reference for guiding participation is the quality of community life. Both the conditions of the community for living and the kinds of lives people are living are of interest. Poor housing is not necessarily a sign of undesirable community life, nor is good housing necessarily a sign of desirable community life. Thus the quality of community life could be worse in the suburbs than in the inner city. To make such judgments there should be some idea as to the criteria for good community life. A major criterion is the realization of full human potential. The community conditions mentioned as most appropriate to human fulfillment are openness to and presence of diversity, and the freedom, opportunity, and implementation of self-determination.

The marks of the kingdom on earth then are the evidences of fulfilled lives, observable not only in the individual members, but also in the structures of the community. The kingdom on earth is to be experienced not only in the extraordinary moments of serving and being served, but in every day participation in the full scope of community life. The role of the minister in the participating church is that of "exemplar" of participation. He both exhorts to participation and sets the example for participation. Thus, in his individual activity and in his congregational leadership, he demonstrates by word and action the concept of participation. The inclusive nature of participation requires his involvement in the politicizing as well as sensitizing function. This concept of the church and the ministry is exemplified in the ministers of the most consistent public style, the public/public type.

Among these ministers there is some sense of their own life being an example not only of participation, but of the fulfillment toward which participation is directed. They do not claim to be fulfilled persons; this would violate one aspect of participation, participation in the imperfections as well as the solutions. Rather they are conscious of the possibilities and characteristics of fulfillment, as others may not be. In the same way the congregation also is an example of fulfillment. Thus, while the contributing church is to the larger community as the saved to the unsaved, and the serving church as the blessed to the deprived, the participating church is to the larger society as the aware and motivated to the unaware and unmotivated--aware of and motivated to pursue the possibilities and characteristics of fulfillment.

The concept of the "participating church" is more a logical extension of "loyalty to the kingdom," than of the "American experience." That is, it is loyalty to the kingdom, not necessarily the American experience, that involves the expectation over time of the kingdom coming in the life of the community of living. And where the American experience does not seem to be fulfilling that expectation, the relation of the churches to that arrangement must be reassessed.

The weakness of this concept, as observed in the Chicago sample, is the tendency to limit the community of participation to the local community, and to overlook the need for long range structural images. It is susceptible, too, to the total identification of the church with the community, or community with the church. It would seem that loyalty to the kingdom requires, until that time when the kingdom is fully come on earth, a group which takes as its particular responsibility the embodying and transmitting of the awareness of the possibilities and characteristics of human fulfillment. And this awareness includes the articulation of the kingdom as the "sovereignty of God," and the "reign of Christ," as well as the "kingdom on earth." The church has been that group historically, and in the absence of an alternate group, must continue to be.

## The Public Style and Civil Religion

We also want to deal briefly with a question that has been implicit in what we have referred to as the "public/public" type of minister and the "participating" type of church.

The relevant data are in the theological justifications of the public style. The ministers spoke in terms of general personal and community fulfillment, including the values of freedom and justice, rather than in the traditional confessional terms of personal salvation, justification, and sanctification. Also relevent is the tendency of the public style to be implemented through participation in programs and organizations of inter-denominational and general community membership, rather than of denominational membership.

The question is this: while the public style may be evaluated as appropriate to loyalty to the kingdom of God and therefore to confessional Protestantism, may it perhaps be more appropriate to or be better accounted for in terms of American public religion? Do those who manifest the public style thus move in the direction of becoming ministers of American society rather than of the Christian churches?

There is, of course, a literature on social or cultural religion, which analyzes religion in terms of its function for society. That religion which grounds and maintains the values of a society is the "public religion." There is also a literature on the public religion of America specifically. Niebuhr considers public religion in America to be a deterioration of the Protestant churches' loyalty to the kingdom of God.[1] Mead refers to the "religion of the public welfare" or the "religion of democracy," which has always existed in uneasy tension with the religion of the churches, or "denominational religion."[2] Robert Bellah, a sociologist, speaks of a "civil religion" which is independent of yet compatible with the religion of the churches.[3]

Regardless of what it is called or how it is analyzed, there is a religious dimension to American society which has both legitimated and been legitimated by the churches, and yet which is not identical to the religion of the churches. This public religion or (adopting Bellah's term) civil religion has a theology, the basic doctrine of which is "trust in deity." The doctrines of "an assurance of reward and punishment" and "a moral order of freedom, equality and justice" are also included.[4] It also has a mission, the extension of the benefits of freedom, equality, and justice to all its citizens, and even to the rest of the world. Further it has a mission structure, the main component of which is the duly constituted government, supported and complemented by other societal components, including the churches.

Is it this civil religion that the public style of ministry tends to serve, rather than the religion of Protestant Christianity? Obviously those ministers whom we have typed as public/public in style have rejected the priority of the goals of denominational maintenance and expansion for the churches' mission. Thus they have rejected that position which defines confessional loyalty in terms of loyalty to a particular denomination. The ministers whom we have typed parochial/public are in a more ambivalent position in relation to their denominations. They are careful of their denominational responsibilities, yet ready in varying degrees to subordinate them to more general and inclusive responsibilities. It is in the parochial/parochial type of minister that Christianity in its denominational particularism is most evident. Is their ministry then, together with that of the more denominationally careful ministers of the parochial/public type, a more legitimate ministry of the Christian church than that of the public/public type of minister?

The marked convergence between the public style of ministry and civil religion is in definition of mission. Both the public style and civil religion define mission in terms of a very this-worldly personal and community fulfillment. There is also a convergence in conception of mission structure--in its broadest statement. The public style, too, sees the structure as inclusive of more than the churches themselves; it is open to the possibility of any societal component being a part of that structure, including duly constituted government.

On the other hand, to the extent that civil religion has tended to institutionalize the mission structure in the established political, economic, and religious structures, the public style cannot be said to serve the civil religion. For the public style, as we have defined it theoretically and observed it in practice, places greater emphasis on the mission potential of the grass-roots oriented political, economic, and religious structures. Thus the public style stands in opposition to not only denominational Christianity but also civil religion.

The public style also diverges from civil religion in the matter of theology. While the public style along with civil religion assumes (as we have noted earlier in this chapter) affirmation of the sovereignty of God, it maintains that the unique motivating and enabling power of the church is the presence and conscious awareness of Jesus Christ and the continued working of the Holy Spirit. Jesus Christ and the Holy Spirit, and the transcendent dimension of life which is implicit in their presence, function as instrumental to, rather than the goal of mission, however.

This is, of course, consistent with the civil religion which assumes that the Christian particularity will be instrumental to the societal mission. But this confessional position causes the public style ministers to say "No" to the actual working out of the societal mission, and to advocate selective participation in established society. Therefore, it cannot unqualifiedly be said to serve civil religion, in its institutionalized form.

We conclude then, that while in its appearance the public style may suggest affinity with American civil religion, in its theology and its conception and carrying out of mission there are significant divergences. The public style is not fully consistent with either denominational Christianity or civil religion. In fact, it may well be that the parochial/parochial style of ministry is most consistent with civil religion. This style tends to confine the explicitly Christian project within parochial boundaries; it tends to affirm less critically not only the intention but the actual working out of the societal mission; and it tends to work within the established mission structure of civil religion.

As the parochial/parochial ministers affirm and take their place within civil religion, at the same time attending to the denominational interests of maintenance and expansion, they may be said to be the ministers of civil religion in effect, while the public/public type are so only in appearance. In this sense, denominational Christianity becomes the "established church" of American society, that which legitimates and is legitimated by society.

If the public style is not fully consistent either with denominational Christianity or American civil religion, with what conception of religion is it a consistent expression? It is like denominational Christianity in that it is confessional; it is unlike it in that it is ecumenical. It is like American civil religion in that it identifies mission with personal and community well-being; it is unlike it in that it stands against established society in both its critical and constructive effort. It is thus a public-oriented religion, with an ecumenical-confessional foundation.

As such it could be said to be a re-emergence of that dynamic stream which Niebuhr identifies as the Protestant movement in America, a stream which is characterized not by denominational particularity or uncritical public functionalism, but rather by loyalty to the rulership of God as it is worked out in societal life. The affirmation of the sovereignty of God, which is also a part of civil religion, is the center which not only legitimates those structures which acknowledge that sovereignty, but places under judgment those which do not. The reign of Christ in the hearts and lives of individuals is the peculiar motivation and staying power which the churches bring to the task. The kingdom on earth is the end toward which they move.

There are two major implications of this thrust for Protestantism in America. The first is that the competitive spirit which has undergirded the recruitment drive of the churches in America is lost when denominational lines are removed. Can this competitive spirit be compensated for by a spirit in which the drive for recruitment is provided by the unfinished business of personal and community fulfillment? Is concern for the well-being of this world as powerful an attracting force as concern for one's own well-being in the world to come? An attraction of the early church appears to have been the way the Christians loved each other; will the way Christians love the world be equally attractive? The present public concern for the environment may indicate an at least temporary affirmative answer to that question.

The second implication is that this thrust of Protestantism severely strains the legitimation of the churches by established American society. The legitimation represented by legal concessions to the churches and by generalized public affirmation of the churches is presently being reconsidered. The question raised is whether or not the churches can survive without that legitimation, and even more basically are they willing to take the risk? The public style could be a test of the limits to the independence allowed the churches within the "lively experiment" of religious freedom and of the churches' willingness to sacrifice their present legitimation for the sake of independence for mission.

The consideration of these implications must include the fact that there are major church bodies in America which as denominations appear to affirm rather fully the established arrangement of denominational Christianity and American civil religion. The so-called "evangelicals," among whom the Lutheran Church-Missouri Synod is sometimes numbered, would be examples of such bodies. If the public style gains ground in the other church bodies, it may well be that the more "sect-like" denominations will become the new established church, and thus fall heir to the social legitimation withdrawn from the old church establishment. This has implications not only for the status of public style churches in American society, which is ultimately a matter of indifference in terms of confessional loyalty, but also for the influence of these churches in American society, which is of tremendous import in terms of mission.

Of course, this consideration of implications is based on a relatively small number of pastors, the public/public group. Yet the question as to whether or not this is the way the churches and their ministry ought to move must be asked, and to answer it these implications must be considered. Then too, we have stated that the tendency in the largest group of ministers, the parochial/public group, is also in that direction, and that only the parochial/parochial group generally conforms closely with the established American arrangement of church and society.

It is then a question of more than academic interest. We have identified this as an actual thrust in American Protestantism. We are further saying that especially those denominations in which the public style is most present must consciously deal with the matter of whether or not this is the direction in which the churches ought to move, to the extent that that movement is susceptible to decision and implementation.[5]

The net effect of this additional consideration of the kingdom of God theme appears at this point simply to reaffirm the Niebuhr hypothesis. The difference is that now it has also been considered against the "civil religion" theme, and been judged still to prevail as an adequate interpretive theme for what is going on in American Protestantism.

Does the present church situation have nothing new to add then? It is the conclusion of this writer, on the basis of the data presented in this study, that the center, the motive, and the end of the churches have not substantively changed, at least in their overt expressions. That is, they continue to be the sovereignty of God, the reign of Christ, and the kingdom on earth. The new overt dimension is probably the manner and degree to which the viability of this informing framework is being tested in response to a new societal situation. We have suggested that the appearance and substance of the ministry which is responding to this situation is consistent with that framework, as the full implications of that framework within contemporary society become apparent.

Nevertheless, the testing of the framework in response to the changing situation may finally prove it to be inadequate and demand something entirely new in the way of conceptualizing the center, motive, and end. The movement out of the churches entirely, particularly of clergy, is an indication that some are already reaching that conclusion. It might be suggested that the public/public type of ministry is just one step removed from such an action. Almost by definition those who remain within the institutional church retain hope for and commitment to it and the possibilities of its informing framework. The validity of this hope and commitment could perhaps be tested by a follow-up of these ministers within the next few years to see where they are in relation to the institutional church, and, by extension, to its confessionally defined center, motive, and end.

### The Local Community and the Local Community Congregation

In this study the local neighborhood and the local community congregation have been treated as "givens." They are a part of the situation within which the role of the minister, the subject of our research, is carried out. The question of the continued viability of the local neighborhood as the unit for citizen membership and participation in an urban society, and of the neighborhood church as the unit of church membership and participation is not specifically within the province of the monograph. Yet their viability is currently being questioned, and it is appropriate that the questioning be acknowledged. Furthermore our research does provide data for some reflection on that question.

At the outset it can be stated that neither the local community nor congregation should be considered as <u>the</u> unit of participation. Local community participation is dependent upon or at least interdependent with larger and more distant decision-making and implementing units. And it is often the case that these larger and more distant units not only have greater authorized power, but greater financial and material resources, and greater access to technical assistance. Thus if effective local control is to be realized, in either church or community, local participation must be extended into these larger units.

Representation is one means of participation, but direct participation is more effective. The exertion of local pressure on outside agencies and interests is another strategy for inserting local interests into the decision-making and implementing process. In the long-run, however, the structuring of local interests into that process would seem to be preferable as the "norm." Local people, serving at the direction of fellow local people, on the various boards and agencies of church and municipality, and local voices in the policy-making of business and industry in the community, are examples of this.

The interests of the local community and congregation also need the broadening which participation in larger units brings. Interests of local units generally are centered on the needs and concerns of family, home, and individual well-being as defined by the particular neighborhood or congregation. In a metropolitan area especially, there are other legitimate interests to be taken into consideration, and a variety of community situations. There is the possibility of a parochialization of the local units in relation to their metropolitan units, just as there is of the sub-units in relation to the local unit.

Nevertheless, our research suggests that the local community and the local community church can each be considered as <u>a</u> unit of participation. Neighborhoods do continue to function as meaningful units of living in the metropolitan area. The interests of family, home, and individual well-being are legitimate interests within the collectivity of metropolitan interests. Specific localities do have their peculiar needs and opportunities which are not taken into consideration as a matter of policy by central decision-making units. In very practical terms the local community and local congregation provide the basic membership and financial bases of the larger units.

What we are suggesting then is a plurality of units of membership and participation in church and society, with the local congregation and local community as necessary and legitimate units within that plurality. The question is not whether but how these two smaller units function in the general pattern of church and community membership and participation. Or what are the needs and functions of church and society to which these units have the capacity for contributing?

We can focus our reflections on this question by referring again to the concepts of the "self-transforming society," and "loyalty to the kingdom of God." The concept of the self-transforming society and that of the kingdom of God are inclusive concepts: they refer to totalities rather than units within totalities. Yet the units constitute and contribute to the totality.

One of the requirements for the self-transforming society is the ability of the central decision-making and implementation units to decide and implement without having to achieve a new consensus for each decision. This ability presupposes a sensitivity to the needs and desires of the constitutive units and a record of taking those needs and desires into consideration. Thus its politicizing function as a whole is legitimated to the constitutive units. This involves a regular and reliable flow of information from the constitutive units to the politicizing group, and of interpretation of action from the politicizing group to the constitutive units.

The local community would seem to be an appropriate unit for the origin of such information and the communication of such interpretation. A city councilman or alderman who spends most of his time at city hall and returns occasionally to the local community contributes to but is not sufficient for this process of information and interpretation. Some organization which operates continuously at the local community level, such as a local community organization, would seem to be a useful complement. In this sense the community organization contributes primarily to the sensitizing and legitimating function.

The local congregation could participate in the sensitizing and legitimating process in cooperation with the community organization. The churches might take as their particular responsibility, the guaranteeing of the participation of the unpropertied and inarticulate in the deliberations and voice of the community organization.

Should the politicizing function then be reserved to the central decision-making and implementation unit? The self-transforming society requires a central policy-making and resources-mobilizing and allocating agency. At the very least the local units must have direct representation in this agency. But beyond this it is possible and feasible to share the politicizing function with the local units. A share of the metropolitan funding could be allocated to the local units for expenditure. The decision and implementation involved in applying centrally-made policy to specific localities might also be delegated to the local unit. Public education and urban development would be two examples of programs in which the local unit can share in the politicizing function. Public transportation and pollution control would be examples of programs better reserved entirely to the central agency, again provided there is direct local representation.

In relation to the church and "loyalty to the kingdom of God" the local congregation is presently the chief expression of the institutional church. As Niebuhr points out in The Kingdom of God in America, however, institutionalization results eventually in the allocating of prime interest and energy to the maintenance of the institution rather than to the cause for which it was established. This has been pointed out to be true of the local congregations, in the literature of the 1960's. There has been conjecture, therefore, as to whether the local congregation ought not be supplanted by other forms with less institutional baggage to carry. Meanwhile congregations might share in the task of "loyalty to the kingdom" by providing financial and manpower support for discovering and establishing the new forms.

Our research indicates that most ministers do not feel this negatively about the congregation. They have hopes that it can make a more positive and direct contribution, and in some cases they are actually demonstrating that this is possible. What is not clear from our research is the long term viability of these efforts. Our hypothesis is that in order to demonstrate "loyalty to the kingdom" as the "kingdom on earth," a more public style of community participation is necessary. We have seen that style among the ministers. But the examples in our research are all relatively recent in origin. They have not proved their capacity to survive in the face of continued demands for the more parochial style, nor to be viable alternatives for maintaining the congregational financial and membership base.

It may be that the parochial demands will in time prevail once more. Or it may be that the public style will entail the sacrifice of the local congregation. On the other hand, the public style may be the means to a new style of congregational form and life that will not supplant or destroy the congregation, but transform it. The matter of what will happen and how it will happen remains to be seen. Some suggestions as to the continued function of the local congregation can be made, begging those other questions for the time being.

To the extent that people are present and available in the community of residence, the local congregation can be a place of gathering and proclamation, of exhortation, and implementation in the task of "loyalty to the kingdom." To the extent that the community of residence is the place of experiencing and responding to human need, the local congregation is "on the scene" for interpreting and initiating response to those needs. To the extent that the community of residence is one dimension of the kingdom of earth, the local congregation is present to anticipate, identify, and cooperate with its coming.

These are positive areas of contribution to the kingdom for which the local congregation is suitably located. The term "to the extent that" indicates, however, that the community is neither the only place that people are present and available, nor the only place where human need is experienced and responded to, nor the full dimension of the kingdom on earth. Therefore, however the local congregation functions, it must be as a part of a larger strategy.

The local congregation as presently structured may not be the best form for the functioning of the church in the local community. For example the structure ought to be such that the ministers and membership are free to move beyond that structure in their community participation. The model of the self-contained congregational structure ought to be re-evaluated in the light of this. A structure which depends on its own organization for all leadership, program, and support components, will consume all the time, energy and resources that its membership can provide. Furthermore, these components are duplicated in the multiplicity of local congregations, and to some extent in non-church community agencies and organizations.

Therefore a model of the congregation in which interaction and interdependence with other congregations and community organizations are structured into the congregational organization should be considered. Thus the neighboring congregation and its leadership and the local community organization and its leadership would be considered as part of the congregation's organization for participation and support. In this model the local congregation is a working part of a larger participating whole rather than a self-contained and self-centered entity. This is a model more appropriate both to a "serving" and a "participating" church.

There are of course implications here for ministers of congregations. In this suggested congregational model the individual minister would be relieved both of the burden impressed from without, and the illusion nurtured from within, that he is a "self-contained" leader, one who possesses the total leadership requirements for a congregation which is "loyal to the kingdom." To function in this model of a congregation, the minister must be trained to get the most from his own particular skills, and those of his fellow ministers, not to mention those of his lay colleagues.

## Education for Ministry

The content and process of seminary education thus comes under consideration. Seminary education has tended to be evaluated by noting whether it developed dependence or independence in its students. While the former has often been the outcome, it is not ordinarily the intention. But the latter is perhaps equally dysfunctional in urban congregations. Interdependence of leadership ought to be the goal, interdependence in relation both to lay people and fellow ministers. Projects which enable the recognition and utilization of special talents or skills in self and others ought to be a part of the educational method. Experiences in which the failure and success of individual efforts contribute to the failure or success of the group also should be provided.

The theological task is one of integration. Ministers are forced by their situations to do business with the needs of the community. These needs are legitimated by the "kingdom on earth" dimension of "loyalty to the kingdom." But while this legitimation is sensed by most ministers, their conscious theological framework will not support wholehearted response. Thus a theological framework in which the "kingdom on earth" is integrated with "the reign of Christ," and the "sovereignty of God" is necessary. This will help provide the ministers with the necessary intellectual grounding for participation in the kingdom's coming in the concreteness of the local community.

Within this framework, the theme of the "kingdom on earth" must be followed through to specific images and models appropriate to the kingdom and applicable to the local and larger community. Congregations must continue to be problem- and issue-oriented; but they must also begin to anticipate problems before they become unmanageable and to capitalize on opportunities. Thus there must be vivid images and models not only of "need" or "sickness" but also of "strength" and "health."

Skills for identifying and responding to both needs and possibilities should also be a part of seminary education. Our sample of ministers expressed the need for community analysis and organization training. Some of this training can be accomplished through classroom and field education. Specific needs in this area are very much a matter of the situation in which the man ministers, however. Therefore, the general training which is a part of the seminary education must be supplemented by training opportunities available after seminary. Consultation in the place of ministry would seem to be more desirable than returning to the seminary or other non-local center.

## Summary

We are inclined to affirm the continued possibilities of the local community and the local congregations and their professional ministers for contributing to the self-transforming society and loyalty to the kingdom of God. But to realize those possibilities, these entities must be considered according to their own characteristics. This means that the local community must be considered not as the whole of community, but as a specific component of the larger community. The local congregation must likewise be considered as a particular form of the larger church, and the parish ministry as one specialty in professional church leadership.

## NOTES AND REFERENCES

### Chapter I


1. Cf. Scott Greer, The Emerging City, Free Press Paperback (New York: The Macmillan Company, 1965), ch. 1.

2. e. e. cummings, "Pity the Poor Monster," quoted in The Climate of Faith in Modern Literature, Nathan Scott, (ed.) (New York: The Seabury Press, 1964), p. 147.

3. Amitai Etzioni, "Toward a Theory of Societal Guidance," American Journal of Sociology, LXXIII (September, 1967), 173-187.

4. H. Richard Niebuhr, The Kingdom of God in America, Harper Torch Books (New York: Harper and Brothers, 1959), p. 24.

5. Ibid., p. 27.

6. Ibid., p. 43.

7. Ibid., p. 51.

8. Jerald Brauer, Protestantism in America (Rev. ed.; Philadelphia: Westminster Press, 1965).

9. Ibid., p. 269.

10. Ibid., p. 278.

11. Ibid., p. 279.

12. Ibid., p. 303.

13. Peter Berger and Thomas Luckmann, The Social Construction of Reality (Garden City, New York: Doubleday & Company, Inc., 1966), p. 113.

14. Sidney Mead, The Lively Experiment (New York: Harper and Row, 1963), p. 58.

15. Ibid., p. 157.

## Chapter II

1. Hospital Planning Council for Metropolitan Chicago, "Median Family Income in 1966 and the Economic Rank of 250 Communities in Metropolitan Chicago," Chicago, April, 1967, pp. 3-15 (mimeographed).

2. Evelyn M. Kitagawa and Karl E. Taeuber, (eds.), Local Community Fact Book: Chicago Metropolitan Area, 1960 (Chicago: Community Inventory, University of Chicago, 1963), p. xiii.

3. Ibid., p. xiv.

4. Leo Burnett, Metamorphosis Chicago Style (Chicago: Leo Burnett Company Inc., 1965), pp. 34-35.

5. Charles Cleveland, "Illinois Politics," in Kloetzli, Chicago Lutheran Planning Study, I, 6:3 [sic].

6. Study by Hospital Planning Council for Metropolitan Chicago, reported in Chicago Sun-Times, January 13, 1967, p. 4.

7. Henry Clark, Manpower for Mission (New York: The Council Press, 1967), p. 7.

8. Bureau of Research, Research Report No. 2-1167 (Chicago: Church Federation of Greater Chicago, n.d.), Table CPGC-1.

9. Further considerations regarding research design, together with the research instruments, are included in the Appendices.

10. Research Department, Chicago Community Area Profiles (Chicago, Welfare Council of Metropolitan Chicago, November, 1964), pp. 159-164.

11. Northeastern Illinois Planning Commission, Metropolitan Planning Guidelines (Chicago: Northeastern Illinois Planning Commission, 1965), Figure A3.

12. The complete instruments are included in Appendix B.

## Chapter III

1. For number of ministers upon which percentages are based, cf. Appendix A, p. 110.

2. Designations "Q" and "I" with a number following, indicate the question(s) from the questionnaire (Q) or interview (I) upon which conclusions and tables are based (see Appendix B for the instruments).

3. In the tables which follow N = 105, distributed as follows: "high" communities = 29; "middle" communities = 56; "low" communities = 20.

4. In this section "N" equals only the number of ministers responding to the particular instrument involved. Where the instrument is the questionnaire, N = 99, distributed as follows: Episcopal ministers = 12; Lutheran Church in America ministers = 19; Lutheran Church-Missouri Synod ministers = 14; Methodist ministers = 21; United Church of Christ ministers = 18; and United Presbyterian ministers = 15. Where the instrument is the interview schedule, N = 102, in which case the distribution is 13, 20, 16, 22, 15, 16, in the same order. The appropriate "N" will be noted in each table.

## Chapter IV

1. Chicago Sun-Times, June 4, 1967, p. 1.

2. Chicago Sun-Times, August 13, 1967, p. 5.

3. Summary of statistical material in Richard A. Cook, South Holland, Illinois: A History 1946-1966 (South Holland: South Holland Trust and Savings Bank, 1966).

4. Ibid., p. 91.

## Chapter V

1. Niebuhr, The Kingdom of God in America, especially ch. V.

2. Mead, The Lively Experiment, especially ch. IV, and "The Post-Protestant Concept and America's Two Religions," Religion in Life, XXXIII (Spring, 1964), pp. 191ff.

3. Robert Bellah, "Civil Religion in America," Daedalus, Vol. 96 (Winter, 1967), pp. 1ff.

4. These specific wordings of the theology are those of Gibson Winter in his preface to The Free Church and Seductive Culture (Scottdale, Pa.: Herald Press, 1970), by Calvin Redekop.

5. It is interesting and perhaps significant to note that four of the denominations in our sample, Episcopal, Methodist (now United Methodist), United Church of Christ, and United Presbyterian, were the four largest members of the nine denomination Consultation of Church Union, and that the preliminary proposal for a new "The Church of Christ Uniting" seems to have taken into consideration the characteristics of the public style as we have outlined and documented it. The church's mission is stated as follows: "The affirmation of Christ's Lordship over creation, including the secular city, must be related to the real struggles of the people in the social, economic, and political structures of this day." Time, March 2, 1970, p. 48.

## APPENDIX A

## METHODOLOGICAL CONSIDERATIONS

The methodological considerations for the research project include the technical ones of adequate research design. But there are theoretical considerations prior to and conditioning these. They can be introduced by reference to the research experience itself.

### Prior Considerations

The primary source of our data was parish ministers. As we talked with the ministers two questions about the nature and purpose of research in relation to the project at hand were asked:

1. How is what you are doing going to help us?

2. How can you get a true picture of the church with these methods?

The first question deals with the value of objective research for the committed participant. The second with the appropriateness of the scientific methodology for the description, evaluation and planning of the program of the church with its unique characteristics.

One detects behind these questions a feeling that the ministers and their churches have not benefited from past research: that they have been "used" to further the private interests of researchers; that research has not been responsibly used by church agencies; that they are weary of hearing, on the basis of "research," that the ministry is an incompetent, disintegrated, or at best confused vocation. Many ministers indicated that they are quite aware of problems in their vocation, that they are seeking to respond constructively to the situation, and that now they need research that will both indicate this and help them in their project of bringing new clarity, competence, and integrity to the vocation to which they continue to be committed.

The men who designed and carried out the research have had parish experience themselves; and a considerable amount of exploratory study preceded the final study. Therefore these questions had been anticipated, and we felt that they were valid. So a part of the methodological consideration was "making a case" for our project that would include the interests of the respondents as well as those of the researchers.

All of this is not to imply that the ministers were not cooperative with the project; they were extremely cooperative. But the writer is inclined to attribute their cooperation more to their interest in the research area and the desire to "tell their story" than to a conviction concerning the value of research itself--at least for the churches and their ministers. There was no need then to make a case for the area of research. In fact it may well have been the very importance of this area to the ministers that caused them to voice these concerns. What they said, and what we did with what they said, mattered to them.

What is the value of objective research for the committed participant? The researcher must be quite ready to acknowledge that he is present to the respondent primarily as one who receives. The value to the respondent is in the significance of the information he gives and the use to which it is put. Conclusions are being drawn and decisions are being made by agencies other than the minister, which nevertheless affect the minister and the situation in which he is involved. It is to his benefit that these agencies base their conclusions and decisions on the best information possible. The researcher can help to make his case by demonstrating that his instruments get at the kind of information which the respondent considers to be significant for the subject area, and by being able to indicate his lines of communication with relevant agencies.

It is also to the respondent's benefit to have available the thinking and experience of other ministers as a way of broadening, clarifying and evaluating his own thinking and experience. Our respondents, for example, were interested in how other ministers had answered the questions we asked. Yet a third benefit to the minister as committed participant is the structured process through which he is asked to communicate his experience and thinking. Again some of our respondents said that they found it helpful to think through this familiar area within the framework of the research instruments. The committed participant thus can benefit from the objective preparation of the researcher, as well as the analysis and communication of research findings.

There is, we conclude, a convergence of the interest of the researcher to discover, order, analyze, and communicate the experience of the committed participant, and the interest of the respondent in his participant role.

What is the appropriateness of the scientific methodology to the church as a subject of research? This question seems to be based on an assumption that research is focused upon the highly relative, ambiguous, and ephemeral data of human projects, structures, and articulations, while the essence of the church and its ministry is a consciousness of and loyalty to a uniquely durable, clear, and transcendent foundation and mandate, the Word and will of God. There is also an assumption that research implies a highly intentional and calculating form of planning and leadership, while the planning and leadership of the church should be open to the spontaneity and guilelessness elicited by the promptings of the Spirit. An incompatibility between subject matter and methodology is suggested.

In responding to this concern, we acknowledge the necessity of investigating an institution or a role in its uniqueness as well as in its sameness, in relation to other institutions and roles, and that the uniqueness of the church and its ministry is in its peculiar relation to the Word and will of God. But we also assert that the historical witness to that Word and will, the Bible and the history of the church itself, testifies to their dynamic character and immanently revealed content. Furthermore the dynamic and immanent is not contradictory but complementary to the durable and the transcendent. Systematic research into the "everyday" dimensions of the church then becomes instrumental to the necessary sensitivity to the dynamic and the immanent.

In addition, while spontaneity and guilelessness are appropriate to religious leadership, responsible leadership requires a clarity of situation and consequence which calls for a high degree of intentionality and calculation. Nor is this contradictory, but rather complementary to these other aspects of religious leadership. The relationship must inform both the carrying out of the research and the use of the findings--which involves both the researcher and the decision-makers.

Therefore, two criteria of reliability were presented for the preparation and implementation of our study: reliability in relation to the methodology used; reliability in relation to the nature of the subject of study. It does not necessarily follow that the case would be different for other areas of research. The intention here has been to show how these concerns were expressed by our respondents and thought through for our project.

One additional consideration is related to these concerns, the communication and utilization of findings. The immediate occasion for this research was a doctoral dissertation. In choosing the area of research it was hoped that it would make a contribution not only to the "sociology of the church," but also to the planning and policy process of the institutions themselves. The ministers, many of them at least, expressed a desire to see the findings themselves and also to put them into the hands of denominational staff. But if no church body has a financial investment in a particular research project, there is no institutional "vested interest" in the research beyond that of individual ministers. Further it would seem that the researcher should take some interest and responsibility in applying the findings to specific institutional problems and opportunities. The methodological considerations of lines of communication and responsibility between independent research and the institutional church remains open for discussion.

## RESEARCH DESIGN

### Research Method

The survey method was chosen as the best way of getting a fairly broad sampling within the limits of available resources. The persons in whose role we were interested would describe their own actions and give their own thinking about the actions. Reliability in this method requires candidness and objectivity on the part of the respondents, and the ability of the researcher to grasp objective experience through the words of the respondent. The researcher must already know something about the activities to which the respondents will be referring: ecumenical parishes, community organizations, human relations commissions, ministerial associations.

On the whole we felt that most ministers, having agreed to participate in the survey, were as thorough and accurate in their responses as possible. We had two means of testing this general confidence in the respondents. The first was our general knowledge of the things that ministers were engaged in in the sample areas, on the basis of the preliminary study. We could compare what we were told with what we already knew. The second was the sampling of ministers by community areas, which resulted in a number of ministers referring to the same situation and activity. Therefore we could also check the responses of one minister with those of others.

We felt we had reliability within the limits of the survey method. Nevertheless the study could have been made more comprehensive by including such methods as direct observation of the ministers' activity, listening to or reading their sermons, and surveying congregation and community members.

### Sample Selection

The first decision was to confine the research to the Chicago metropolitan area. While limited in scope, this sample was accessible. Furthermore, we felt that the community situations in which Chicago ministers carry on their ministries have similarities with those of ministers across the country. In addition, our familiarity with Chicago led to the assumption that if the kind of experience we were hypothesizing were to be found at all, it would be present there. If the hypotheses were found to be largely validated, it would be worthwhile to test them further in other areas; on the other hand, if they were discovered to be largely invalidated, we would not expect to find them significantly validated in other areas.

Details on the sample selection are included in Chapter II. As might have been surmised, our "human welfare needs" indices for typing communities came very close to the Social Areas Analysis index of "social rank." Use of the Shevky-Bell criteria for social rank, resulted in a very similar distribution of communities: a "high" welfare need community is one of "low" social rank. And it was also the case that almost all of the "high" communities were close to 100 percent Negro in population. Since we did not have exactly equivalent data on the suburban communities, we included in the "low" category the newer, higher social rank suburbs. The selection was not random; but it was apparent that our subject matter and our resources would not lend themselves to conclusions based solely on tests of statistical significance. Therefore we felt free to employ our own knowledge to assure a variety of community situations.

### Instruments

The function of the instruments was to get as much data as possible about the minister's participation in his community, in both its operational and theoretical dimensions. We wanted data applicable to the testing of our hypotheses. We wanted data which the respondents would feel were adequate to their own understanding of what they were doing and why. We wanted to account for the institutional base of the role we were studying, which meant allowing for a theological directive, and for particular organizational requirements and limitations upon the role.

It was decided that a pre-coded, forced-response questionnaire could provide data on a number of items which are statistical in nature or which can easily be reduced to a fixed number of alternative answers. The complete questionnaire is included in Appendix B. A second instrument was a structured, open-response interview schedule. This instrument is also included in Appendix B.

Prior to construction of the instruments we attempted to work out typologies of theo-sociological orientations to be built into the instruments. This proved an extremely complex task to do abstractly, and assumed that concrete individual thinking can be fit into mutually exclusive and exhaustive theological categories and cross-tabulated with similarly neat sociological categories. On the basis of our own presuppositions about human individuality, this was not a valid assumption. Therefore, although we developed tentative typologies and constructed the instruments so that they could emerge if actually present, the provision was made for emergence of alternative possibilities.

An example of the provision for alternative possibilities are the several Likert-type scales in the questionnaire which we thought might discriminate between "conflict" and "consensus" orientations to social organization and change. Then in the interview we asked the minister to describe how he analyzed and responded to actual social situations, which allowed us to suggest the minister's "working" orientation. Thus we also provided for the probability that ministers must often decide and act before they have fully explored the theoretical implications of what they are about. A number of ministers, when pressed for theological grounding, stated that they had not done this task as yet; but almost all felt that such grounding was implicit in what they were doing.

Because both of the instruments focused on the one area of community-centered ministry, we had the problem of putting community activity into its proper perspective with the total ministry. It might appear that this was the most important aspect of ministry for the individual minister, while in reality consuming a small proportion of his time. In order to meet this problem one question asked for a ranking of community activity in relation to other functions, and another asked for a percentage-of-time estimate. In addition the final question of the interview asked the minister what he considered to have been "most significant" in his total ministry during the past year. It was at this point that many of the ministers pointed out that while the social problems of the community had absorbed a great deal of their time, it was the more "pastoral" activities of counseling, hospital visitation, etc., that proved the most satisfactory.

## Sample Response

The tables below give a statistical summary of the sample selection and response.

Of the 105 ministers who responded, 6 responded in the interview only, giving us a total of 99 questionnaires, and 3 responded in the questionnaire only, giving us a total of 102 interviews.

TABLE 35

SAMPLE SELECTION AND RESPONSE BY TYPE OF COMMUNITY

| | Sample Selected | | Sample Responding | |
|---|---|---|---|---|
| Type of Community | Number | Percentage of Total | Number | Percentage of Total |
| High | 39 | 28.2 | 29 | 27.6 |
| Middle | 71 | 51.5 | 56 | 53.4 |
| Low | 28 | 20.3 | 20 | 19.0 |
| Total | 138 | 100.0 | 105 | 100.0 |

TABLE 36

SAMPLE SELECTION AND RESPONSE BY DENOMINATION

| | Sample Selected | | Sample Responding | |
|---|---|---|---|---|
| Denomination | Number | Percentage of Total | Number | Percentage of Total |
| Episcopal | 16 | 11.6 | 13 | 12.4 |
| Lutheran (LCA) | 23 | 16.7 | 20 | 19.0 |
| Lutheran-Missouri Synod | 25 | 18.1 | 17 | 16.2 |
| Methodist | 31 | 22.5 | 22 | 21.0 |
| United Church of Christ | 22 | 15.9 | 18 | 17.1 |
| United Presbyterian | 21 | 15.3 | 15 | 14.3 |
| Total | 138 | 100.0 | 105 | 100.0 |

Of the 33 ministers from whom no response was gained, pastoral vacancies accounted for 19, there was no contact made with 5, 6 ministers refused outright, and 3 made and then cancelled appointments.

## Date of Research

The exact historical context into which the research reported in this **monograph** should be placed is May-June, 1967. The research was preceded by observation of and participation in the Chicago church-community situation beginning in October, 1963. The research was designed during the first part of 1967, with the actual administering of the research instruments taking place during May and June of that year. In a rapidly changing church-community picture, it is important that these months be kept in mind as the "present" which is referred to in the **monograph.**

## Statistical Significance

The intention of the research, as noted in the **opening chapter,** was to explore rather than to prove a hypothesis. This was based both on the nature of the subject matter and the limitation of our resources. Furthermore, it will have been noted that the sample selection was not entirely random. Our sample was selected then, not to enable us to draw conclusions on the basis of tests of statistical significance, but to enable us to talk about the ministry in specific areas with a considerable degree of confidence, and to compare the ministers in similar areas. Beyond that, in the tables, we have been able to indicate tendencies of a variety of factors to be associated with the kind of participation of ministers in their communities, which one would at least be justified in looking for in areas not included in the sample.

While our conclusions have been based primarily upon tendencies directly observable in the presentation of research data, we have nevertheless included the results of tests of statistical significance in many of the tables in Chapter IV. The tests are to see if the relation indicated between the respective variable and the specific factor (type of community, denomination, public or parochial style) is significant or random. Where the tests were made, the test statistic, the degrees of freedom, and the level of significance (if significant at all) are included.

Almost all of the tests are the chi square test of significance. The Kolmogorov-Smirnov test, however, was used in the tables comparing the "public" with the "parochial" style. The small number of cases expected in some of the cells, particularly where the factor being tested is that of denomination (six columns), made it necessary to combine some rows, or to eliminate some altogether (e.g., the "no reply," "blank" columns) to get a valid test. Where the logic of the variable discriminations did not allow for this, or where the responses are overwhelmingly in one row no test statistic is reported at all. Where a test is not reported, therefore, it is either not possible, given the data, or considered not particularly relevant to the given table.

In general then, where a test is reported it is to be understood as an additional observation about the sample itself. Application of significance to a larger universe is to be done only within the limitations noted above.

The tests of statistical significance do tend to validate the conclusions regarding the weight of the "community factor" in determining the degree of the "public style" and of the "denominational factor" in determining the degree of the "parochial style." For example the following observations about the significance of the "high" welfare need community for the public style are all supported by statistical tests which are significant at the .05 level or better.

1. There are community areas in which the ministers perceive a multiplicity of problems affecting human welfare, which make those areas below average in terms of their general "livability."

2. Ministering in these community areas includes an added dimension in preaching and teaching, namely emphasis on "members' responsibility in community life" and on the "large social issues of the day." It also involves a higher priority for community activity, both in actual time spent and relative to other aspects of ministry.

3. A cause of community problems, especially significant in these community areas, is the arrangement or distribution of power, which finds the residents of the community on the short end. Consistent with this is the participation of ministers in these communities in the problem of community representation through parapolitical types of activity, especially through the agency of the local community organization. Ministers in these areas affirm the greater effectiveness of these organizations, particularly in reference to their competence in getting things accomplished, i.e., effectively addressing the imbalance of power.

4. Ministers in these areas tend to manifest the transformative orientation to community problems, i.e., their assessment of and response to community problems can be summarized as emphasizing the prior necessity of changing the arrangement of power, to give greater voice to the needs of people in the community.

The following observations can be made in relation to the significance of the denominational factor for the parochial style, supported by statistical tests which are significant at the .05 level or better.

1. The parochial preaching and teaching emphasis on the "inner life," with a corresponding lack of emphasis on "community responsibility" and "large social issues" is significant for the Lutheran Church-Missouri Synod ministers. Likewise the lowest ranking (fourth) for community activity is related to these ministers.

2. Ministers of this denomination show the greatest variance, on the low side, in participation in parapolitical activity, in participation in some kind of community association other than the congregation, and in taking some position on organizing local residents for action.

3. The more parochial-related orientations to community problems, the accommodative and assertive, are found more among the Missouri Synod ministers (also United Church of Christ), while the more public-related transformative orientation is found among the Lutheran Church in America, Methodist, and United Presbyterian ministers.

Therefore, although the tests of significance are not the primary basis for conclusions about the hypotheses, they do tend to strengthen the conclusions made.

## APPENDIX B

## SURVEY INSTRUMENTS

### Parish Ministry Survey

### A Questionnaire

Instructions:

Most of the questions to follow can be answered by checking or circling the appropriate answer. There are only a few questions where written answers are requested. However, feel free to note any comments or qualifications in the left margin as you go along.

This questionnaire is confidential. Your answers will not be identified with your name or that of your congregation in any report based on this survey.

The numbers in the right margins next to the answer categories are only an aid to tabulation. Please disregard them in answering questions.

* * * * * * * * * * * * * * * * * * * * * * * * * * * * * * * * * * * * * * *

LET'S BEGIN WITH A FEW QUESTIONS ABOUT YOUR CONGREGATION. PLEASE PLACE A CHECK MARK NEXT TO THE ANSWER WHICH APPLIES.

1. What is the approximate total confirmed membership of the congregation?
   - Less than 150 . . . . . . . . . . . . . . . . . ______1
   - 150-299 . . . . . . . . . . . . . . . . . . . ______2
   - 300-499 . . . . . . . . . . . . . . . . . . . ______3
   - 500-999 . . . . . . . . . . . . . . . . . . . ______4
   - 1000 or more . . . . . . . . . . . . . . . . . ______5

2. About what percentage of the adult members of the congregation is over 50 years of age?
   - Less than 25% . . . . . . . . . . . . . . . . . ______1
   - 25%-49% . . . . . . . . . . . . . . . . . . ______2
   - 50%-74% . . . . . . . . . . . . . . . . . . . ______3
   - 75% or more . . . . . . . . . . . . . . . . . ______4

3. About what percentage of the adult members of the congregation is <u>blue collar in occupation</u>?
   - Less than 25% . . . . . . . . . . . . . . . . . . ____1
   - 25%-49% . . . . . . . . . . . . . . . . . . . . ____2
   - 50%-74% . . . . . . . . . . . . . . . . . . . . ____3
   - 75% or more . . . . . . . . . . . . . . . . . . ____4

4. About what percentage of the adult members of the congregation has had <u>2 years or more of college education</u>?
   - Less than 25% . . . . . . . . . . . . . . . . . . ____1
   - 25%-49% . . . . . . . . . . . . . . . . . . . . ____2
   - 50%-74% . . . . . . . . . . . . . . . . . . . . ____3
   - 75% or more . . . . . . . . . . . . . . . . . . ____4

5. What is the racial makeup of the adult membership of the congregation?
   - All Negro. . . . . . . . . . . . . . . . . . . . ____1
   - Mostly Negro . . . . . . . . . . . . . . . . . . ____2
   - About half Negro and half White. . . . . . . . ____3
   - Mostly White . . . . . . . . . . . . . . . . . . ____4
   - All White . . . . . . . . . . . . . . . . . . . ____5

   If there are White members, do they tend to represent a particular ethnic group?
   - No . . . . . . . . . . . . . . . . . . . . . . . ____1
   - Yes . . . . . . . . . . . . . . . . . . . . . . ____2
     (please specify____________________________

6. About what percentage of the membership of the congregation live <u>within one mile</u> of the church building?
   - Less than 25% . . . . . . . . . . . . . . . . . . ____1
   - 25%-49% . . . . . . . . . . . . . . . . . . . . ____2
   - 50%-74% . . . . . . . . . . . . . . . . . . . . ____3
   - 75% or more. . . . . . . . . . . . . . . . . . . ____4

7. What has been the membership trend during the past five years?
   - Membership has been decreasing . . . . . . . . ____1
   - Membership has remained about the same . . . ____2
   - Membership has been increasing . . . . . . . . ____3

8. If there has been an increase in membership, what do you feel are the reasons? (Check as many as apply)
   - Newcomers to neighborhood are interested in church participation . . . . . . . . . . . ____1
   - Gain in population in the neighborhood . . . ____2
   - Change in religious makeup of the neighborhood . . . . . . . . . . . . . . . . ____3
   - Good church program. . . . . . . . . . . . . . ____4
   - Vigorous evangelistic and recruitment efforts . . . . . . . . . . . . . . . . . . ____5
   - Approval of pastor's theological and social views . . . . . . . . . . . . . . . . ____6
   - Other (please specify)____________________________7

9. If there has been a decrease in membership what do you feel are the reasons? (check as many as apply)
   - Newcomers to neighborhood are not interested in church participation . . . . . . . . . . . _____1
   - Loss of population in neighborhood . . . . . . _____2
   - Change in racial makeup of neighborhood . . . . _____3
   - Change in socioeconomic level of neighborhood . _____4
   - Poor church program . . . . . . . . . . . . . . _____5
   - Members have moved away . . . . . . . . . . . . _____6
   - Poor evangelistic and recruitment effort. . . . _____7
   - Disapproval of pastor's theological and social views . . . . . . . . . . . . . . . _____8
   - Other (please specify)_____________________________9

10. In which of the following stages is the congregation in its building program? (check as many as apply)
    - Mortgage paid in full . . . . . . . . . . . . . _____1
    - Paying off mortgage . . . . . . . . . . . . . . _____2
    - Planning for new construction or major renovation . . . . . . . . . . . . . . . . . _____3
    - New construction or major renovation now in process . . . . . . . . . . . . . . . . . . _____4
    - Other: (specify) . . . . . . . . . . . . . . . _____5

11. Does the congregation receive financial aid from your denomination or some other outside source?
    - Yes . . . . . . . . . . . . . . . . . . . . . . _____1
    - No . . . . . . . . . . . . . . . . . . . . . . _____2

12. How long has the congregation been in its present location?
    - Less than 5 years . . . . . . . . . . . . . . . _____1
    - 5- 9 years . . . . . . . . . . . . . . . . . . _____2
    - 10-24 years . . . . . . . . . . . . . . . . . . _____3
    - 25-50 years . . . . . . . . . . . . . . . . . . _____4
    - More than 50 years. . . . . . . . . . . . . . . _____5

    If the congregation was at one time located elsewhere, please give previous location:_____________________________________________

13. Please list on the lines below any community groups to which the congregation has made a financial contribution during the last 12 months (e.g., community organizations, councils of churches, social service agencies, civil rights groups, etc.).

    ______________________________  ______________________________

    ______________________________  ______________________________

BEFORE ASKING ABOUT YOUR MINISTRY, WE WOULD LIKE SOME INDICATION OF YOUR GENERAL VIEWS ON VARIOUS ASPECTS OF COMMUNITY LIFE. FOR QUESTIONS ASKING SPECIFICALLY ABOUT "YOUR COMMUNITY," PLEASE REFER TO THE AREA IN WHICH YOUR CHURCH BUILDING IS LOCATED.

14. By what name is your community generally known to people in the area? Please specify:______________________________

15. Below are listed a number of social problems which are present in various parts of the Chicago area. Please indicate whether in your community, you consider each item to be a serious problem, somewhat a problem, or not a problem (place a check in the appropriate column).

| | Serious problem | Somewhat a problem | Not a problem | Don't know |
|---|---|---|---|---|
| Youth gangs . . . . . . . . . . | ____1 | ____1 | ____1 | ____1 |
| Deteriorating housing . . . . | ____2 | ____2 | ____2 | ____2 |
| Inadequate public education . . . . . . . . | ____3 | ____3 | ____3 | ____3 |
| Police harassment . . . . . . | ____4 | ____4 | ____4 | ____4 |
| Burglary, vandalism, assault . . . . . . . . . | ____5 | ____5 | ____5 | ____5 |
| Ineffective political representation. . . . . . | ____6 | ____6 | ____6 | ____6 |
| Racial prejudice. . . . . . . | ____7 | ____7 | ____7 | ____7 |
| Family instability. . . . . . | ____8 | ____8 | ____8 | ____8 |
| Mental, emotional stress. . . . . . . . . . . | ____9 | ____9 | ____9 | ____9 |

16. Compared with other sections of the Chicago metropolitan area, how would you rate the community as a place to live?
    - Below average . . . . . . . . . . . . . . . . ____1
    - About average . . . . . . . . . . . . . . . . ____2
    - Above average . . . . . . . . . . . . . . . . ____3

17. Try to imagine a ladder with ten rungs. If the top rung (No. 10) represents your idea of the "best possible city" and the bottom rung (No. 1) represents your idea of the "worst possible city," on which rung would you place the city of Chicago today? (circle one number)

1 2 3 4 5 6 7 8 9 10

Where on the ladder would you say the city was five years ago?

1 2 3 4 5 6 7 8 9 10

Where do you think the city will be five years from now?

1 2 3 4 5 6 7 8 9 10

18. Below are listed a variety of organizations which are trying to deal with problems of urban life. In each case please indicate how you feel about their general approach to things.

If you strongly favor the approach, circle "1"
If you favor the approach, but with qualifications, circle "2"
If you have no feelings, one way or the other, circle "3"
If you oppose the approach, but with qualifications, circle "4"
If you strongly oppose the approach, circle "5"
If you are not familiar with the organization, circle "6"

| | Strongly Favor | | | | Strongly Oppose | Not Familiar |
|---|---|---|---|---|---|---|
| Church Federation of Greater Chicago. . . . . . . . . | 1 | 2 | 3 | 4 | 5 | 6 |
| Archdiocese of Chicago . . . . . . | 1 | 2 | 3 | 4 | 5 | 6 |
| Billy Graham Crusade . . . . . . . | 1 | 2 | 3 | 4 | 5 | 6 |
| Your own denomination (synod, diocese, conference, association) . . . . . . | 1 | 2 | 3 | 4 | 5 | 6 |
| Chicago Urban League . . . . . . . | 1 | 2 | 3 | 4 | 5 | 6 |
| Black Muslims . . . . . . . . . . | 1 | 2 | 3 | 4 | 5 | 6 |
| Southern Christian Leadership Conference (SCLC) . . . . | 1 | 2 | 3 | 4 | 5 | 6 |
| Student Nonviolent Coordinating Committee (SNCC) . . . . . . . . . . . . | 1 | 2 | 3 | 4 | 5 | 6 |
| Coordinating Council of Community Organizations (CCCO) . . . . . . . . . . . . | 1 | 2 | 3 | 4 | 5 | 6 |
| Chicago Conference on Religion and Race. . . . . . . | 1 | 2 | 3 | 4 | 5 | 6 |
| Young Men's Christian Association. . . . . . . . . . | 1 | 2 | 3 | 4 | 5 | 6 |
| Lions, Kiwanis . . . . . . . . . . | 1 | 2 | 3 | 4 | 5 | 6 |
| Operation Breadbasket. . . . . . . | 1 | 2 | 3 | 4 | 5 | 6 |
| The Woodlawn Organization (TWO) . . . . . . . . . . | 1 | 2 | 3 | 4 | 5 | 6 |
| West Side Organization (WSO). . . . . . . . . . . . . | 1 | 2 | 3 | 4 | 5 | 6 |
| Metropolitan Chicago Leadership Council for Open Housing. . . . . . . . . . . . | 1 | 2 | 3 | 4 | 5 | 6 |

19. The following items are statements of attitude or evaluation, to which you are asked to agree or disagree. For each statement please circle the number which most nearly represents your own view.

If you are in <u>strong agreement</u>, circle "1"
If you <u>tend to agree</u> but not emphatically, circle "2"
If you are <u>almost neutral</u> but <u>probably agree</u>, circle "3"
If you are <u>almost neutral</u> but <u>probably disagree</u>, circle "4"
If you <u>tend to disagree</u> but not emphatically, circle "5"
If you are in <u>strong disagreement</u>, circle "6"
If you feel unable to indicate any degree of agreement or disagreement, circle "7" for "uncertain."

| | Strong Agreement | | | Strong Dis-agreement | | | Uncertain |
|---|---|---|---|---|---|---|---|
| Things are pretty good nowadays, so it is best to keep things the way they are. | 1 | 2 | 3 | 4 | 5 | 6 | 7 |
| Whether we like it or not the city is really dominated by powerful interest groups. | 1 | 2 | 3 | 4 | 5 | 6 | 7 |
| Man deserves from society only what he earns by his own efforts. | 1 | 2 | 3 | 4 | 5 | 6 | 7 |
| America may not be perfect, but the American Way has brought us about as close as human beings can get to a perfect society. | 1 | 2 | 3 | 4 | 5 | 6 | 7 |
| The ideal residential community consists of people with similar backgrounds and interests. | 1 | 2 | 3 | 4 | 5 | 6 | 7 |
| Public officials are more responsive to the claims of social justice than the possibilities of political advantage. | 1 | 2 | 3 | 4 | 5 | 6 | 7 |
| Every man has a right to the best living conditions that his society can provide. | 1 | 2 | 3 | 4 | 5 | 6 | 7 |
| In city planning the judgments of experts should have priority over the desires of people in local neighborhoods. | 1 | 2 | 3 | 4 | 5 | 6 | 7 |
| In community affairs most people are guided in their decisions by what is best for the whole community. | 1 | 2 | 3 | 4 | 5 | 6 | 7 |

Many religious leaders have said that race relations is one of the most serious problems facing the churches of the Chicago area. As we continue with your community views we ask how the problem of race relations relates to your particular situation.

20. Do you think the major religious denominations in Chicago should be doing more than they are currently doing to reduce racial prejudice?

Yes, Chicago churches should be doing more. . . . . . . . . ._____1
No, Chicago churches should be doing less . . . . . . . . . ._____2
No, Chicago churches are currently directing about the
    right amount of effort to this problem. . . . . . . . ._____3

21. Since last summer, has your denomination started a program to reduce prejudice and discrimination in the Chicago area?
    Yes . . . . . . . . . . . . . . . . . . . . . . . . . ._____1
    No . . . . . . . . . . . . . . . . . . . . . . . . . ._____2
    Don't know. . . . . . . . . . . . . . . . . . . . . . ._____3

22. In the past six months, has the subject of racial prejudice and discrimination been discussed in any of the following ways? (check as many as apply)
    Sermons . . . . . . . . . . . . . . . . . . . . . . . ._____1
    Small group meetings. . . . . . . . . . . . . . . . . ._____2
    Films, guest speakers . . . . . . . . . . . . . . . . ._____3

23. In your opinion, how successful would a well designed educational program to reduce prejudice and discrimination be in your congregation? (check <u>one</u>)

Probably would reduce prejudice and discrimination for
most members of the congregation. . . . . . . . . . . . . ._____1

Probably would produce both positive and negative changes,
but more positive than negative . . . . . . . . . . . . . ._____2

Probably would produce both positive and negative changes,
but more negative than positive . . . . . . . . . . . . . ._____3

Probably would not have much effect, one way or
the other . . . . . . . . . . . . . . . . . . . . . . . . ._____4

Such a campaign would only harm the congregation by
stirring up trouble . . . . . . . . . . . . . . . . . . . ._____5

24. On the whole, how do you think your congregation feels about open housing? Most members of the congregation are: (check <u>one</u>)
    Extremely opposed . . . . . . . . . . . . . . . . . . ._____1
    Moderately opposed. . . . . . . . . . . . . . . . . . ._____2
    Unconcerned . . . . . . . . . . . . . . . . . . . . . ._____3
    Moderately favorable. . . . . . . . . . . . . . . . . ._____4
    Extremely favorable . . . . . . . . . . . . . . . . . ._____5

NOW LET US TURN TO YOUR MINISTRY. THE NEXT SET OF QUESTIONS ASKS ABOUT SOME OF THE WAYS IN WHICH YOU RESPOND TO NEEDS AND OPPORTUNITIES PRESENT IN URBAN SOCIETY.

25. Urban pastors differ in the relative importance they give to their various responsibilities. Please indicate the relative position you give to the following responsibilities.

In the FIRST column indicate their relative position according to the importance you think they ought to have. (Please rank 1 to 4: "1" for the most important, "2" for the next most important, etc.)

In the SECOND column indicate the position they actually have in the amount of time you give them. (Please rank 1 to 4.)

In the THIRD column indicate the position they have according to the degree of personal satisfaction you receive from them. (Please rank 1 to 4.)

| | Ought to have | Actually have | Satis-faction |
|---|---|---|---|
| Preaching, teaching, public worship . . . . . . . . . . . . . . . . | ____ | ____ | ____ |
| Pastoral calling and counselling . . . . . . . . . . . . . . | ____ | ____ | ____ |
| Administrative work | ____ | ____ | ____ |
| Community activity . . . . . . . . . . . | ____ | ____ | ____ |

26. As you think about your preaching and teaching, what emphasis do you find yourself giving to each of the following subjects? (Check for each subject whether you give much, some, little, or no emphasis.)

| | Much Emphasis | Some Emphasis | Little Emphasis | No Emphasis |
|---|---|---|---|---|
| Inner-life of faith and devotion . . . . . . . . . . | ____1 | ____1 | ____1 | ____1 |
| Interpersonal and family relations . . . . . . . . . . | ____2 | ____2 | ____2 | ____2 |
| Members' occupational life. . . . . . . . . . . . . . | ____3 | ____3 | ____3 | ____3 |
| Members' responsibility in community life . . . . . . . | ____4 | ____4 | ____4 | ____4 |
| Large social issues of the day. . . . . . . . . . . | ____5 | ____5 | ____5 | ____5 |

27. If you were to be given a choice of type of ministry, which of the following would you most prefer? (check one)

| | |
|---|---|
| Minister in "inner city" parish (i.e. among the poor) . . . . | ____1 |
| Minister in city parish, other than "inner city". . . . . . . | ____2 |
| Minister of suburban parish . . . . . . . . . . . . . . . . . . | ____3 |
| Minister of town and country parish . . . . . . . . . . . . . | ____4 |
| Military or institutional chaplain. . . . . . . . . . . . . . | ____5 |
| Teacher in college or seminary. . . . . . . . . . . . . . . . | ____6 |
| Community service or action leader. . . . . . . . . . . . . . | ____7 |
| Denominational staff position . . . . . . . . . . . . . . . . | ____8 |
| Other: (please specify)________________________________ | ____9 |

28. Would you say the above choice represents a change from your present type of ministry?

Yes, a change . . . . . . . . . . . . . . . . . . ._____1
No change . . . . . . . . . . . . . . . . . . . . ._____2

29. With how many of the other clergymen in your community would you say you have a personal acquaintance?

All or nearly all . . . . . . . . . . . . . . . . ._____1
About half . . . . . . . . . . . . . . . . . . . ._____2
Only a few . . . . . . . . . . . . . . . . . . . ._____3
None . . . . . . . . . . . . . . . . . . . . . . ._____4

30. What does your association with other ministers in your community tend to center around? (Write "1" beside the subject which receives the greatest emphasis, and write "2" beside that which receives the next greatest emphasis.)

Fellowship. . . . . . . . . . . . . . . . . . . . ._____
Theological and professional concerns . . . . . . ._____
Community issues. . . . . . . . . . . . . . . . . ._____
Inter-church programs . . . . . . . . . . . . . . ._____
Other: (please specify)_______________________________

31. Many controversial issues are currently being discussed in the Chicago area. Would you please indicate whether or not you support each issue in the list below (check "yes" or "no"), and indicate whether you have publicly made known your support or lack of support, in sermon, church meeting, newsletter, community group, press, speech, etc. (check "yes" or "no"). If you are undecided on the issue, check "undecided," or if you are not familiar with it, check "don't know."

| | Support Yes | Support No | Publicly Yes | Publicly No | Undecided | Don't Know |
|---|---|---|---|---|---|---|
| Guaranteed annual income | __0 | __0 | __0 | __0 | __0 | __0 |
| Maintaining the neighborhood school policy | __1 | __1 | __1 | __1 | __1 | __1 |
| Statewide open occupancy law | __2 | __2 | __2 | __2 | __2 | __2 |
| Air pollution control | __3 | __3 | __3 | __3 | __3 | __3 |
| Organizing relief recipients into welfare unions | __4 | __4 | __4 | __4 | __4 | __4 |
| Public demonstrations for peace in Vietnam | __5 | __5 | __5 | __5 | __5 | __5 |
| Regional planning for metropolitan development | __6 | __6 | __6 | __6 | __6 | __6 |
| Organizing local residents for a greater voice in community decision making | __7 | __7 | __7 | __7 | __7 | __7 |
| Negro housing protest demonstration marches in white neighborhoods | __8 | __8 | __8 | __8 | __8 | __8 |
| Organized violence as a strategy for social change | __9 | __9 | __9 | __9 | __9 | __9 |

32. In thinking about your response to local community problems, which of the following actions have you engaged in during the last year? (check as many as apply)

Spoken about specific community issues from the pulpit . . . ____1
Encouraged members of congregation to take action, through study groups or individual conversation . . . . ____2
Written letters to public officials. . . . . . . . . . . . . . ____3
Informal visits with public officials or other community leaders. . . . . . . . . . . . . . . . . . . . . . ____4
Personally worked for a particular candidate or referendum in an election. . . . . . . . . . . . . . . . . ____5
Helped organize community groups to take action. . . . . . . ____6
Participated in civil rights demonstrations, picketing, boycotting or other forms of direct action . . . . . . . ____7
Other: (please specify)________________________________8

33. Pastors in metropolitan areas participate in a wide variety of associations outside their local congregation. In the spaces below please list all such organizations, committees, boards, and ad hoc groups of which you are now an active participant. (e.g., community organizations, service clubs, local clergy groups, denominational assignments, and so on)
Place an "x" after those in which you hold an office. Please be as specific as possible--when in doubt as to whether or not an association is applicable here, include it.

________________________ ________________________

________________________ ________________________

________________________ ________________________

________________________ ________________________

34. Has your experience in the ministry made you feel the need for any types of training in the seminary program that were not available when you were a student?
No . . . . . . . . . . . . . . . . . . . . . . . . . . ____1
Yes. . . . . . . . . . . . . . . . . . . . . . . . . . ____2
(please specify)____________________________

35. The following items are more statements of attitude or evaluation to which you are asked to agree or disagree. For each statement please indicate the position on a six point scale which most nearly represents your own view by circling the appropriate number.

If you are in strong agreement, circle "1"
If you tend to agree but not emphatically, circle "2"
If you are almost neutral but probably agree, circle "3"
If you are almost neutral but probably disagree, circle "4"
If you tend to disagree but not emphatically, circle "5"
If you are in strong disagreement, circle "6"
If you feel unable to indicate any degree of agreement or disagreement, circle "7" for "uncertain"

| | Strong Agreement | | | | Strong Dis-Agreement | | Un-certain |
|---|---|---|---|---|---|---|---|
| One's relation to God is immediate and direct and has nothing to do with relationships with other people. | 1 | 2 | 3 | 4 | 5 | 6 | 7 |
| The Christian faith provides clear-cut answers to contemporary ethical questions. | 1 | 2 | 3 | 4 | 5 | 6 | 7 |
| The most creative and exciting forms of ministry are found in inner-city parishes. | 1 | 2 | 3 | 4 | 5 | 6 | 7 |
| The working of God can be seen in the human struggle for freedom and dignity. | 1 | 2 | 3 | 4 | 5 | 6 | 7 |
| Responsible Christians should not enter into the give and take of political compromise. | 1 | 2 | 3 | 4 | 5 | 6 | 7 |
| In civic and political matters a minister should: | | | | | | | |
| Act on behalf of his congregation | 1 | 2 | 3 | 4 | 5 | 6 | 7 |
| Prepare and encourage members of the congregation to act individually | 1 | 2 | 3 | 4 | 5 | 6 | 7 |
| Encourage the congregation to take corporate action | 1 | 2 | 3 | 4 | 5 | 6 | 7 |
| Act along with the congregation | 1 | 2 | 3 | 4 | 5 | 6 | 7 |
| Act only as a private citizen. | 1 | 2 | 3 | 4 | 5 | 6 | 7 |

36. Admittedly, there are difficulties associated with describing oneself in terms of broad theological positions. However, within the following categories, which of the following best describes your own theological position?

Fundamentalist . . . . . . . . . . . . . . . . . . . ____1
Conservative . . . . . . . . . . . . . . . . . . . . ____2
Neo-orthodox . . . . . . . . . . . . . . . . . . . . ____3
Liberal. . . . . . . . . . . . . . . . . . . . . . . ____4
Other . . . . . . . . . . . . . . . . . . . . . . . ____5
(please specify)____________________________________

FINALLY, A FEW QUESTIONS ABOUT YOURSELF.

37. What is your age?
Under 35 . . . . . . . . . . . . . . . . . . . . . . ____1
35-44. . . . . . . . . . . . . . . . . . . . . . . . ____2
45-54. . . . . . . . . . . . . . . . . . . . . . . . ____3
55-64. . . . . . . . . . . . . . . . . . . . . . . . ____4
65 or over . . . . . . . . . . . . . . . . . . . . . ____5

38. In what kind of community did you spend the majority of your grade and high school years?
Rural. . . . . . . . . . . . . . . . . . . . . . . . ____1
Small town (under 25,000 population) . . . . . . ____2
City (25,000 to 100,000 population) . . . . . . ____3
Metropolitan (over 100,000 population) . . . . ____4
Urban area . . . . . . . . . . . . . . . . . . ____5
Suburban area . . . . . . . . . . . . . . . . . ____6

39. What is your educational background?

| | Institution | Last Year Attended | Degree |
|---|---|---|---|
| College | ____________ | ________ | ______ |
| Seminary | ____________ | ________ | ______ |
| Postgraduate | ____________ | ________ | ______ |

(postgraduate field)____________________________________________

40. What other formal training have you had within the past five years (institutes, workshops, seminars, etc., totaling at least 12 hours each)? (check as many as apply)
Preaching . . . . . . . . . . . . . . . . . . . . . ____1
Christian Education. . . . . . . . . . . . . . . . ____2
Pastoral Counseling. . . . . . . . . . . . . . . . ____3
Worship and Music. . . . . . . . . . . . . . . . . ____4
Community Organization . . . . . . . . . . . . . . ____5
Specific Social Problems . . . . . . . . . . . . . ____6
Urban Training Center. . . . . . . . . . . . . . . ____7
Ecumenical Institute . . . . . . . . . . . . . . . ____8
Other (please specify)____________________________9

41. Which of the following best describes your position before coming to your present parish?

Minister in "inner city" parish (i.e., among the poor) . . . . . . . . . . . . . . . . . . . . . . . ____1
Minister in city parish, other than "inner city". . . ____2
Minister of suburban parish . . . . . . . . . . . . . . . . ____3
Minister of town and country parish . . . . . . . . . . ____4
Military or institutional chaplain . . . . . . . . . . . ____5
Teacher in college or seminary . . . . . . . . . . . . ____6
Community service or action leader . . . . . . . . . . ____7
Denominational staff position . . . . . . . . . . . . . . ____8
Other (please specify) ________________________________9

42. How long have you been in your present pastorate?
Less than six months. . . . . . . . . . . . . . . . . . . ____1
Six months to one year . . . . . . . . . . . . . . . . . ____2
1-3 years . . . . . . . . . . . . . . . . . . . . . . . . . ____3
4-5 years . . . . . . . . . . . . . . . . . . . . . . . . . ____4
6-10 years . . . . . . . . . . . . . . . . . . . . . . . . ____5
More than 10 years . . . . . . . . . . . . . . . . . . . ____6

43. Approximately how far is your home from your church?
Less than ½ mile . . . . . . . . . . . . . . . . . . . . ____1
½ mile to 1 mile . . . . . . . . . . . . . . . . . . . . ____2
1-2 miles . . . . . . . . . . . . . . . . . . . . . . . . . ____3
2 or more miles . . . . . . . . . . . . . . . . . . . . . ____4

This is the end of the questionnaire. Thank you for your participation.

# PARISH MINISTRY SURVEY

Interview Schedule[1]

Introduction: In our interview we have a certain number of questions that we'd like to cover in this hour, so I'll move right along from one question to the next. Then at the end, I'll ask for additional comments that may have come to your mind.

1. The purpose of our study is to find out what parish ministers consider to be the mission needs and opportunities in their communities, and how they are responding to them. To begin, it would be helpful if you would tell me something about this community--in particular what are the problems that cause you the greatest concern?

   Probe: Are there any other problems that concern you?

2. (if more than one problem) Which of these problems seem of greatest urgency to you?

3. Do you have any thoughts concerning the basic causes of this problem? or (if no "most urgent" specified): Let's take the problem of ______________. Do you have any thoughts concerning the basic causes of this problem?

4. Are there people in the community who are working at this problem? (specify group, individuals--including the minister, and type of constituency if not obvious in title)

   Probe 1: Are there any others working at it?
   Probe 2: Is anyone working from the other side of the issue?

   (if no one responding): How do you account for the lack of response to the problem?

   Are there other community problems that people are working on? (specify problems, groups, individuals--including minister)

   (if none at all): How do you account for this general lack of response to community problems? [then go to 7*]

---

[1]Spaces for writing answers have been omitted.

5. Of all the groups that you mentioned which would you say has been most effective in dealing with the problem?

<u>Probe 1:</u> What are the reasons for its effectiveness?
<u>Probe 2:</u> Are you pretty much in agreement with the way this group works at the problem?

(If only one group--person--mentioned in No. 4, substitute for 5 and 6): How effective has this group been in dealing with the problem?

<u>Probe:</u> What are the reasons for its effectiveness (or lack of effectiveness)?

(If minister's individual response proceed to No. 8)

6. Which of these groups has been least effective in dealing with the problem?

<u>Probe:</u> What are the reasons for its lack of effectiveness?

7. a. You mentioned that you are involved in________________________ group or program:

<u>or</u>
b. Are you personally involved in any of the groups working at the problem?

(b. only) _____yes: specify

(a. and b.) (if more than one) In which of these have you been investing the most time?

Why have you chosen to participate in this particular group? (Or, if does not wish to specify "most time" take <u>community organization</u> type if possible, and continue)

(if not "most" or "least" effective above): How effective has this group been in dealing with the problem?

<u>Probe</u>: What are the reasons for its effectiveness (or lack of effectiveness)?

(*b. only) _____ no: Is there a particular reason why you are not participating in any of them? (specify)

Are there any community groups or projects in which you do participate?

_____ yes: specify (if more than one): In which of these have you been investing the most time?

What would you say is the primary purpose of this group?

How effective has it been in achieving its purpose? (probe for reasons)

_____ no. If your congregation were located in a community where most of the people were living in poverty conditions--poor income, poor housing, poor health, do you think you would be more likely to be involved in community activities than you are here?

_____ yes, more likely

_____ no.

(record any comments, proceed to No. 12*)

When you are asked by members of the congregation to explain the connection between______________________ (problem and/or activity) and the work of the church, how do you answer?

(if never asked): How would you explain it if you were asked?

Probe 1: Are there specific theological doctrines or biblical teachings that help you make the connection between______ and the work of the church?

Probe 2: Is your understanding of the concept of "God's saving work" at all related to this activity?

Do you feel in community activity that you contribute something as a minister that laymen are unable to contribute? (specify)

In thinking about the various community groups or activities in which you participate, would you say you are more or less involved than you were 5 years ago? (if out of seminary less than 5 years: --than you were in your last parish, or--than you expected you would be?)

_____ about the same: Would you say that community conditions are about the same as they were five years ago?

_____ yes, the same
_____ no, different: How do they differ now?

_____ more or _____ less active now: How do you account for the difference?

On an average, about what percentage of your "working time" is taken up by your community activity?

_____ 10%; _____ 10-19%; _____20-34%; _____ 35-49%; _____50-74%;

_____75+%

12. Have the members of the congregation expressed themselves concerning your community activity--the amount of time you spend this way, the stands you've taken, or your being involved at all?

* Have the members of the congregation given any expression of their feelings about the minister's being involved in community issues or activities?

_____ yes: specify (including proportions)

_____ no: Do you have any impression of their feelings? (specify, including proportions)

13. What seems to underlie this response of the members?

Probe: Are you aware of any outside interest groups which are influencing the response of your members?

(if any disapproval) How have you handled the disapproval?

14. Do people of the community seem to be more or less supportive of your community activity, than members of your congregation?

_____ about the same

_____ more or _____ less supportive: How do you account for the difference?

15. (unless specified in 13, 14) Have you, or any other pastors in the community, received any pressure or offer of favor from outside interest groups, in connection with community activity or stands that have been taken? (specify)

16. Do the other ministers in the community tend to see the community situation pretty much the same way you do, and support similar kinds of activity?

_____ only a few agree; _____ most agree; _____ about half agree.

Do those who have a different point of view from you have anything in common with each other?

(ask only in Negro or integrated communities) Is there any cooperation between ministers of predominantly white denominations and those of predominantly Negro denominations in your community?

_____ yes: specify

_____ no: Why do you think this is so?

17. In your ministry here, do you feel that you are moving along the same lines as your denomination?

_____ yes, same lines: What forms of support and encouragement do you receive from the denomination?

_____ no, different lines: Does the denomination try in any way to get greater conformity of your ministry to their expectations? (specify)

18. Most ministers encourage their members to become involved in community problems as individual Christians. Do you encourage the congregation as a whole, or groups within the congregation, to deal with community problems?

    _____ yes: Why do you encourage this?

    Probe: Do you feel that as a church group they have special resources to contribute or draw upon for dealing with community problems?

    _____ no: What are your reasons for not encouraging this?

19. (if not answered previously) Is your congregation as a whole, or are groups within the congregation dealing in any way with community problems? (specify)

20. There is one problem that seems to be of widespread concern these days, that we are asking all of the ministers to comment on--the problem of poverty. Why, in general, do you think we have a poverty problem?

21. In considering the poor people, what kinds of help would you say they are most in need of?

22. Is the problem of poverty at all present among the members of your congregation?

    Probe: In what way and to what extent?

23. Which of the programs presently dealing with poverty do you feel is most effective?

    Probe: What are the reasons for its effectiveness?

24. Which of the programs do you feel is least effective?

    Probe: What are the reasons for its lack of effectiveness?

25. Are there some particular theological doctrines or biblical teachings that help you interpret the problem of poverty, and decide what needs to be done about it?

    (if not: What guidelines help in your interpretation?)

26. What about the local churches or denominations? Do you think they ought to be doing something in relation to this problem? (specify)

27. In the interview we've been looking mainly at one particular aspect of your ministry here. Now looking at your ministry as a whole, what do _you_ consider to have been _most significant_ in your ministry during the past year?

    _Probe 1_: Why do you feel this is significant?

    _Probe 2_: Do your members also see this as something significant?

28. That was the last of the interview questions. Is there anything you would like to add or comment on, either from the interview or the questionnaire?

# BIBLIOGRAPHY

## References for the Conceptual Framework of the Monograph


Bellah, Robert. "Civil Religion in America." Daedalus, Vol. 96 (Winter, 1967), 1-21.

Bellow, Saul. Herzog. Fawcett Crest Books. Greenwich, Conn.: Fawcett Publications, Inc., 1965.

Berger, Peter and Luckman, Thomas. Social Construction of Reality. Garden City, N. Y.: Doubleday and Co., 1966.

Brauer, Jerald. Protestantism in America. Revised ed. Philadelphia: Westminster Press, 1965

Dewey, John. The Public and Its Problems. Denver: Allan Swallow, 1927.

Etzioni, Amitai. "Toward a Theory of Societal Guidance." American Journal of Sociology, LXXIII (September, 1967), 173-87.

Greer, Scott. The Emerging City. Free Press Paperback. New York: Macmillan Co., 1965.

Mead, Sidney. The Lively Experiment. New York: Harper and Row, 1963.

________. "The Post Protestant Concept and America's Two Religions." Religion in Life, XXXIII (Spring, 1964), 191-204.

Niebuhr, H. Richard. The Kingdom of God in America. Harper Torch Books. New York: Harper and Brothers, 1959.

Scott, Nathan A., Jr., ed. The Climate of Faith in Modern Literature. New York: Seabury Press, 1964.

Winter, Gibson. "Preface" to Calvin Redekop, The Free Church and Seductive Culture. Scottdale, Pa.: Herald Press, 1970.

## References for the Field Research of the Monograph

Bruckner, D. J. R. "Richard J. Daley Is:." Los Angeles Times, August 18, 1968 ("West" section magazine), 12-17.

Burnett, Leo. Metamorphosis Chicago Style. Chicago: Leo Burnett Co., Inc., 1965.

Bureau of Research. "Research Report No. 2-1167." Chicago: Church Federation of Greater Chicago, n.d. (Mimeographed.)

________. "Research Memo." Chicago: Church Federation of Greater Chicago, August, 1965. (Mimeographed.)

Chicago Sun Times. Articles, October 19, 1966; January 13, June 4, August 13, 1967.

Clark, Henry. Manpower for Mission. New York: Council Press, 1967.

Community Renewal Program. People, Jobs, and Homes. Chicago: City of Chicago, June, 1963.

Cook, Richard A. South Holland, Illinois: A History, 1946-1966. South Holland, Ill.: South Holland Trust and Savings Bank, 1966.

Department of City Planning. Basic Policies for the Comprehensive Plan of Chicago. Chicago: City of Chicago, August, 1964.

Hospital Planning Council for Metropolitan Chicago. "Median Family Income in 1966 and the Economic Rank of 250 Communities in Metropolitan Chicago." Chicago, April, 1967. (Mimeographed.)

Kitagawa, Evelyn M., and Taeuber, Karl E., eds. Local Community Fact Book: Chicago Metropolitan Area, 1960. Chicago: Community Inventory, University of Chicago, 1963.

Kloetzli, Walter, ed. Chicago Lutheran Planning Study. Vol. I. Chicago: National Lutheran Council, 1965.

Northeastern Illinois Planning Commission. Metropolitan Planning Guidelines. Chicago: Northeastern Illinois Planning Commission, 1965.

Research Department. Chicago Community Area Profiles. Chicago: Welfare Council of Metropolitan Chicago, November, 1964.

Sauter, Van Gordon. "The Changing City: A Series." Chicago Daily News, May 9-11, 1967. (Reprint.)

Vise, Pierre de, compiler. Basic Planning Studies on Metropolitan Chicago. Chicago: Hospital Planning Council for Metropolitan Chicago, April, 1965.